Divorce by Design

Empowering yourself through conscious choices

By Elizabeth Fairon

The material in this book is provided for information purposes only. The reader should consult with his or her personal legal, financial and other advisors before utilising the information contained in this book. The author and the publisher assume no responsibility for any damages or losses incurred during or as a result of following this information.

There are many legal principles included in this book which the author has explained in her own way. If required, specific references can be provided on request.

All names referred to in this book have been changed to protect the identity of the individual.

Published 2023 by Independent Ink
PO Box 1638, Carindale
Queensland 4152 Australia

© Elizabeth Fairon 2023

The moral right of the author has been asserted.

All rights reserved. Except as permitted under the *Australian Copyright Act 1968*, no part of this book may be reproduced or transmitted by any person or entity, in any form or by any means, electronic or mechanical, including photocopying, recording, scanning or by any information storage and retrieval system, without prior permission in writing from the author.

Cover design by Catucci Design
Back cover photography by Jason Malouin
Typeset in 11/17 pt Bembo by Post Pre-press Group, Brisbane

Cataloguing-in-Publication data is available from the National Library of Australia

ISBN 978-0-6486371-0-3 (pbk)
ISBN 978-0-6486371-1-0 (epub)

*"I can't go back to yesterday
because I was a different person then"*

Lewis Carroll, *Alice's Adventures in Wonderland*

Contents

Introduction 1
    About the Author 4
    Things to Know About This Book 5

Chapter 1: All Aboard ... Welcome to the Rollercoaster 9
    Understanding the Grief Cycle After Divorce 11
    Divorce and Trauma 17
    People React to Divorce Differently 21

Chapter 2: Your Kids Come First 29
    Impact of Divorce and Conflict on Children 32
    Coming Up With a Plan for Your Kids Moving Forward 42
    Co-parenting With a Difficult Ex 52

Chapter 3: Managing Your Money 55
    Assessing Your Financial Circumstances 58
    Create a Budget for Your Current Living Situation 62
    Ways to Generate Income for Your Budget 66
    Understanding Legal Fees 68
    How to Pay for Legal Fees 70
    More Affordable Divorce Approaches 72

Chapter 4: Looking After You 75
    Looking After Your Mind 78
    Looking After Your Body 85
    Looking After Your Spirit 92

Chapter 5: It's No Time for Game Playing 97
    Revenge Is Not the Answer 99
    Don't Be an Ostrich 102

Make Up Your Mind   104

Being Right Isn't the Answer   107

Accept Your Part in the Story   107

You Do Not Know Everything   109

What if Your Ex Doesn't Cooperate?   111

Chapter 6:   Attitude Is Everything   113

Signs That You Need to Shift Your Attitude   115

Maintaining a Positive Attitude   116

Chapter 7:   Helpful People   129

Seeking Financial Advice   131

Seeking Legal Advice   135

Seeking Help from a Professional Counsellor or Therapist   139

Key Points to Remember When Seeking Help   143

Chapter 8:   Rules to Live By   145

Rule 1: Always Do the Right Thing   147

Rule 2: Don't React, Act   150

Rule 3: Pick Your Battles   154

Chapter 9:   The Future Is Yours   159

Finding Happiness and Joy After Divorce   161

Making New Friends After Divorce   164

Reconnecting With Hobbies and Passion Projects After Divorce   166

Learning to Trust Again   169

Conclusion   171

Acknowledgments   173

Author Contact Details   175

Introduction

Do you feel like your life is getting out of control because your marriage has come to an end or is headed in that direction, and now you can't stand the thought or presence of the person you hoped to be with for the rest of your life?

Do you feel like you are on an intense rollercoaster, where despite dealing with your grief, loss, anxiety, and fear, you have to deal with your ex, kids, family, and friends too?

Are you looking for a book that will help make your divorce less dramatic, painful, and overwhelming and guide you on how to move on with life without losing yourself and still manage to be the best parent you could ever be?

If you've answered YES:

You are in the right place because this comprehensive guide has you covered.

People separate for different reasons, and you and your ex-partner probably tried everything before things got to where they are right now. And despite that, it seems the best option is for you to go your separate ways.

Now that one of you has packed their bags, almost everyone seems invested in your life and has become a "marriage counsellor". Some are still hung up on your union and trying to help you work things out, while others tell you to disappear and never look back. All the advice you get daily overwhelms you, and to make matters worse, your kids are probably not handling it well. And as if that's not enough, your ex might be battling mental health issues, personality disorders, narcissistic behaviours, or other unhealthy personality issues, which doesn't make things any easier for you.

With all this happening, you probably are wondering …

What's wrong with me? Why do I behave or feel this way?

Will the kids be okay?

How will I manage the money? Will I be able to afford things?

What if it's too hard to take the high road?

What if my ex starts to play dirty?

Who can I get help from?

Will I be okay in the future?

How do I take care of myself?

It is okay to have all these thoughts, and whether you left, were left, or the decision was mutual, this book will help you make good decisions about how you manage your divorce process, allowing you to come out of it more resilient and wiser than before.

How?

By thinking about the choices that we make in an active, conscious way.

Choice: the act of choosing between two or more possibilities.

To engage in conflict or not.

To respond with outrage or not.

To actively seek out revenge or not.

To look after yourself or not.

In this book, you will find information to help you make conscious choices about managing your divorce. The more aware you are of information and knowledge as it applies to your circumstances, the more empowered you are to make good decisions. You are well-informed. You are aware of the possible outcomes. You make *conscious choices*.

And so in **Chapter One**, you will learn about the *rollercoaster of divorce*, how your emotions play out and how you might react to divorce depending on your personality.

In **Chapter Two**, we'll look at the *impact of divorce and conflict on children* and the steps you can take to help your children cope with change and devise a plan moving forward.

In **Chapter Three**, we do a deep dive into *managing your money*, understanding your assets and debts and managing your budget, now and into the future.

Chapter Four looks at the importance of *looking after yourself* – your mind, your body, and your spirit, to ensure you come through your divorce journey prioritising your well-being.

In **Chapter Five**, we will look at *the games people play*, consciously or subconsciously, and how to avoid playing those or manage the player to move through your divorce process efficiently.

In **Chapter Six**, we will look at the *importance of maintaining a positive attitude*, despite all that is thrown at you, along with tips to shift your attitude.

Chapter Seven introduces you to *helpful people* and the importance of seeking legal and financial advice early on and supporting yourself with a therapist or counsellor.

Chapter Eight sets out three *rules to live by*, especially when things get tough and you are faced with all sorts of bad behaviour from your ex.

Finally, **Chapter Nine** will dive deep into *your future* with some information to help you find happiness and joy after your divorce.

In the **Conclusion**, I pull all the critical information together for you.

Note that this book is written as an information guide only. It should not be read as advice specific to your personal circumstances. You should always consult with a lawyer to obtain legal advice about your individual circumstances. Importantly, as I mention below and several times in this book, ***you should seek advice from a lawyer in your jurisdiction (area)***.

ABOUT THE AUTHOR

I am a Legal Practice Director at Life Law Solutions, a law practice in Queensland, Australia. I've been working with families since I started at this firm back in June 2005. While my legal practice includes other areas, my passion lies in helping families resolve their family law matters as quickly and sensibly as possible so their time and money can be spent on more important things.

I have been working in family law for a long time. It means I go to court when we need to and help clients navigate the court system, which can sometimes be pretty overwhelming. It is something that we try to avoid. If there is an out-of-court solution, this is always my preference.

I also assist the court in complex matters as a lawyer appointed for children – an independent children's lawyer. This is the primary focus of my practice right now. I am prioritising assisting the court in these parenting matters, which is why I can talk to you about my experience with families with children in the divorce system and the impact conflict has on children.

Knowledge and education are my key drivers. If you have practical information about your legal issue, you can be empowered to decide to resolve your matter and find solutions to those legal issues that impact your life.

So what can a lawyer, all the way over in Australia, tell you about family law in other parts of the world? Well, while, yes, the law in each jurisdiction (the area where you live) is different, and the languages we use around the world are different (more about that shortly), I believe some concepts are universal, such as how people behave during divorce and the empowerment that comes from understanding that behaviour so you can make better decisions to benefit specifically your children, but, importantly, also you.

The concepts in this book are not legal principles, and you should talk to a local lawyer about the law. However, family and divorce law is not always only about the law, winning a legal point, or proving a point of "winning" at the end of the day. Family and divorce law is first and foremost about people and families, and that's why having a fundamental understanding of human behaviour will help you make it out to the other end of your divorce journey.

THINGS TO KNOW ABOUT THIS BOOK

There are some important things to know about how I have written this book.

There is no law in this book, no legal principles about how family law matters might work in your area, and no advice about how to do things in certain ways to obtain a strategic outcome. I have written the book in this way for two reasons. Firstly, as I said earlier, this book is about universal principles of human behaviour and how you can make good choices to resolve your divorce for your and your family's benefit. Secondly, it would be impossible for me to write a book that includes references to the law around the world – each country has a different legal system. While there are some similarities, there are no universal legal concepts.

Having said that, there are **some legal words that are important to mention**. Around the world, legal practitioners have different titles. Lawyer, Solicitor, Barrister, Advocate, Attorney, Counsellor, Counsel, Prosecutor, Public Defender, District Attorney. In this book, I have chosen the word ***Lawyer***. Regardless of the title, what you are looking for in a lawyer is someone who has undertaken relevant study to be a lawyer, sat or passed any entrance test or course, and is licensed to practise as a lawyer in your jurisdiction. More importantly, you are looking for a lawyer that practises or specialises in family and divorce law instead of someone who dabbles from time to tie.

Another concept that you hear in divorce law is ***child custody***. Generally, child custody is a concept that refers to where your children live and how you make decisions about them. Physical custody and legal custody are regularly used terms in some jurisdictions. In Australia, our legal system has not used the word "custody" since the 90s. Our current language is around where the children live and how they spend time with each parent. Decision-making is referred to as parental responsibility. So you can see why discussing the law in different jurisdictions is impossible in one book.

In this book, you won't see the word custody. You will see references to ***parenting arrangements***, ***where the children live***, ***and how the children spend time with your ex***. The concepts are the same, just described differently.

Finally, ***the grammar and formatting in this book are in Australian English***. That means – no "z", the occasional "u" thrown in, and some other letters doubled or in a different order. The principles are the same; the words mean the same. Go with it.

It is on that basis that I hope you find this book useful. While it is crucial that you get legal advice about your own individual matter, what you will find in this book is information in a format you can understand to equip you to make good conscious choices to move forward to finding a solution to your family law matter.

Chapter 1:

All Aboard ... Welcome to the Rollercoaster

Yes, divorce is tough on everyone involved, but before we discuss anything, let's put you first. Divorce can take an emotional, financial, physical, and mental toll on you to the point that you might think it has made things worse, when you expected it to improve your life.

In this section, we will learn how divorce affects you, irrespective of whether you are the one who initiated it or not. You will discover the role of your emotions, trauma, grief cycle, and personality in all this, understand why and how it gets worse before it gets better, and get some tips on being ready for the worst.

With that said, let's start your new journey!

UNDERSTANDING THE GRIEF CYCLE AFTER DIVORCE

Nobody gets married only to get divorced later, and that's why you are feeling broken and lost. Divorce can feel like the death of a loved one where you are left devastated, and as such, you will experience grief, or you are probably already in the first few stages.

And even though there is no universally applicable grief cycle, you will go through several emotional stages as you adjust to the end of your marriage. These stages are similar to the well-known *Kübler-Ross model of grief*, which was initially developed to describe the emotional process of coping with the loss of a loved one.

Note: Only some people go through all of these stages, and their order and duration vary from one person to the other.

Stages of the Grief Cycle

Here are the emotional stages that you may experience:

1. Denial

Here, you are in shock and disbelief that your marriage is ending, and to shield yourself from the overwhelming reality, you might use denial as a defence mechanism.

If you are the one who initiated the divorce, you might fall into denial about the reasons behind your decision. For example, if your ex-partner was unfaithful, you may tell yourself there is no way they could have done that to you even though you have all the evidence, which might be even worse if they say they didn't have an affair. On the other hand, if you didn't ask for a divorce, you might face denial by thinking that you can change your ex-partner's mind and work things out.

During denial, you might:

Initially, you might *fail to accept that your marriage has ended* and instead hold onto the hope of reconciliation, believing the divorce is a temporary setback or a mistake. As a result, you will probably avoid discussions about it, whether they are about legal proceedings or ideas on how to move on.

You can **downplay the emotional and practical consequences** of the divorce by convincing yourself that you don't need help to cope with the situation or that the divorce is not a big deal. To minimise the impacts of the divorce, you might make statements like "Marriage is not even that important" or "I'll be okay on my own."

Intense feelings and emotions accompany divorce; you might use denial to suppress or ignore them. You may distract yourself through work or other healthy or unhealthy activities, try to numb your feelings, or avoid reminders that trigger emotional distress. You probably believe your emotions and feelings will disappear if you do not acknowledge them, but this is untrue.

Perhaps you are **maintaining the status quo**, acting as if the marriage is intact and going about your daily routine as if everything is okay and nothing has changed. Are you still wearing your wedding ring, or do you refer to your ex-spouse like you did when married? Or have you kept things the same around the house even though your ex has already moved out?

Well, it's because you are still in denial.

And while you might find relief in denial, it is temporary and unhealthy. It can hinder or prolong your healing process, making it hard for you to move on. Accepting the truth will allow you to move forward if you have established that the separation is final.

2. Anger

Anger is common and expected during a divorce.

During this stage, reality has started to set in; you have realised that you are divorcing, and since divorce is a challenging and emotionally charged experience, you might feel resentment, frustration, and anger towards yourself, your ex-spouse, or the circumstances surrounding the divorce. For example, if you initiated the divorce, you might wonder, *"Why did they cheat on me? Was I not good enough? Why me?"* If your ex-partner initiated it, you might think, *"But why can't they take me back? I showed them how sorry I am."*

Moving past this stage might take a while, and you might fall back into it occasionally. This is especially so if you notice that your ex-spouse has moved on.

Watching yourself feel miserable as the other person leads a happy life can trigger anger, and you might start blaming them for things that aren't even their fault. For example, your car might break down on your way home, and you might say, *"If it were not for so and so, I would have a better car right now."*

I once managed a divorce where one party was stuck in the anger stage for the whole divorce process. They were very bitter and reactive to every aspect, even sensible solutions. I also handled another matter where one party could not accept the relationship was over and let go. The way they saw the settlement was sometimes outside of reality, but they were entrenched and couldn't move forward. What does this tell you? You must learn to manage anger during divorce so it doesn't take control of you and the outcome.

And as much as you want your ex-partner to be miserable, it is essential to remember that everyone's experience is unique. Not all individuals go through the same emotional stages or experience them in the same order. Whether you believe it or not, they are going through the same thing as you, but differently.

3. Bargaining

During this stage of grief, you feel the need to fix things with your ex-partner. You might make deals or try to negotiate to save the marriage or change the divorce outcomes.

You probably have convinced yourself that you will never get anyone better than your ex, that if you avoid and ignore the source of your troubles, you will be as okay and happy as before. As a result, you might find yourself making promises or compromises, hoping to find a way to reconcile or avoid the divorce altogether. For example, say you separated because your partner was unfaithful or had been sober for years and then went on a bender. In these cases, you might demand that they promise never to do that again, and bargain with them and yourself that this can never happen again. If you were the partner in the wrong, you might promise to seek help and set rules and boundaries for your behaviour.

This stage might be challenging, especially if you both experience it simultaneously. You both will want to make things work out, but here is the thing: you probably still need to process and deal with the reason behind the separation, and you need more time to be ready to face and move past the reasons. This stage is just your mind realising that you are separating or getting a divorce and trying to fix things.

It is essential to remember that the bargaining stage is *a natural part of the grieving process* and a reflection of the desire to hold onto what was once familiar and meaningful. And while it is understandable to want to find a resolution or save the relationship, it is essential to approach the bargaining stage with a realistic mindset.

Are the promises you are making or being made to you realistic, or will you create a vicious cycle that will cause more damage? There must have been a good reason one of you asked for the divorce, and if it was mutual, you probably tried some of the things being bargained now, right?

4. Depression

Sometimes, you might wake up in the middle of the night and start crying. And sometimes, you will see a couple holding hands at the movies and feel sad for yourself. Sometimes, you won't feel like getting out of bed; you want to be left alone, lost in your thoughts.

During the depression stage, you will likely lose your appetite, have low energy, experience changes in your sleep pattern, and feel sad, hopeless, and lonely most of the time. Even though you might have known that this stage was coming, you can never be prepared enough. You could stay here for months or even years, and it is possible to go through it only to return to the first two stages and come back.

Yes, cutting ties with your "partner" is hard, and that's why depression may hit hard and sometimes have a repetitive pattern, impacting your growth and progress. Even though it is natural to have most, if not all, of the feelings associated with depression, it is essential that you learn how to manage your emotions for your well-being.

Remember that everyone experiences divorce differently, and the duration and intensity of this stage can vary. If you find that your depression is persistent, significantly impacting your daily functioning or causing thoughts of self-harm or suicide, it is crucial to seek immediate professional help.

5. Acceptance

This final stage of grief entails accepting that you are separated and getting divorced and ready to take the necessary steps to move on with your life. No, this doesn't mean that you will suddenly feel happy. It means you are ready to seek help, talk to someone, and improve your emotional, mental, and physical health.

Sure, you will be sad, angry, or nostalgic occasionally, but the difference is that you will have accepted the reality. You will also be open to letting some people in. Realising that you are not alone is a step toward healing.

During this stage, you will be ready to think about your future and that of your kids without letting your emotions get in the way. You might find yourself going out more, wanting to get some new clothes or a new haircut. Since you might no longer be friends with some of the people you used to hang out with, especially with your ex-partner, you will be ready to meet and make new friends.

This shows that you have started embracing your new reality, can see some light at the end of the tunnel, and believe you can make it.

Remember that grief is a process and it could take time to get to the acceptance stage. Also, it is essential to remember that your journey will be different from that of your ex-spouse, so don't feel bad if they seem to heal faster than you. Be patient and kind with yourself, and let your journey unfold naturally.

DIVORCE AND TRAUMA

Technically, divorce is not defined as a traumatic situation or event. However, some people experience symptoms related to trauma during divorce.

And what is a traumatic situation?

According to the US National Institute of Mental Health, a traumatic situation is a ***scary, emotional, or shocking experience that affects you physically, emotionally, and mentally.*** So, trauma comes from traumatic conditions, such as sexual abuse, severe injury, or any life-threatening event.

But can we say that divorce is a traumatic situation?

If you experience shock or distress after or during a divorce, we could say it is a traumatic experience for you. However, in most cases, these symptoms, which are related to trauma, may not be a result of the divorce itself but due to the circumstances that led to it or are around it. For example, verbal abuse, physical abuse, infidelity, or emotional torture, among other instances, are painful experiences that could lead to divorce, leaving you traumatised. Divorce could also lead to trauma if the grief cycle hits you deeply, leaving you stuck for a while.

Some of the signs and symptoms you may experience if or when your divorce causes trauma include the following:

- Insecurities with existing or new attachments
- Prolonged flashbacks and nightmares
- Unending symptoms of depression
- The development of a personality disorder
- Tantrums and emotional outbursts
- Anxiety
- Post-traumatic stress disorder (PTSD) symptoms
- Avoiding your duties and responsibilities
- Isolating yourself from your loved ones

The degree of trauma after a divorce varies from person to person, depending on factors such as the reasons behind the divorce, the circumstances following the divorce, how long you were married, if there are kids involved, and the level of conflict during legal processes.

However, it is essential to note that **not everyone experiences trauma after divorce**. You will likely navigate the process more efficiently if you are resilient and have a robust support system.

Understanding Your Emotions During Divorce

Divorce often leads to intense, uncomfortable, frightening, and unsettling emotions, thoughts, and feelings, such as sadness, anger, frustration, and grief. You may experience emotions related to loss, betrayal, and failure, which can take time to process and heal.

Here are some of these emotions and their causes:

- The relationship was significant to you, and the thought of losing something that was supposed to last forever may frequently cause guilt and sadness. **Sadness** could be due to the feelings of disappointment and loss caused by the end of dreams and plans that you may never realise. **Guilt** could stem from the thought of all the ways you have failed and the people you have let down. For example, if you relocate, you could feel guilty about changing your children's routines and schedules. Guilt could also manifest if there was a loss of trust or infidelity.
- **Fear and anxiety** are other common feelings during a divorce. First, you are single again and may stay that way for a while or forever, and nobody looks forward to spending the rest of their life alone. Your financial status will likely change, and you might wonder if you will handle all the bills. Co-parenting arrangements and all the legal processes involved in a divorce

can lead to fear of the unknown and stress, translating into anxiety. At the same time, your social and living circumstances will change, and you might find yourself thinking, "Will I lose the couple-friends we had? Will they see me as a failure and want nothing to do with me?"

- You might be *angry* at yourself for failing or at your ex-partner, especially if they were the cause of the separation, and especially if they were abusive, stubborn, and petty, or maybe they betrayed you, leading to the divorce. This can lead to frustration and resentment, causing you to be angry at yourself, the cause of the divorce, or your spouse.

These are just a few emotions you may experience, and they all can make you miserable. Even though these emotions can be painful, they all are natural responses to challenging situations, particularly those associated with loss and grief.

Sure, emotions don't have a cure, but there are healthy coping mechanisms we will discuss later that will help make them less painful and make you strong and compassionate throughout the divorce process.

How Your Brain Responds to the Emotions

During a divorce, the brain plays an essential role in processing and experiencing your feelings and emotions, and it can:

1. Activate the Amygdala

The amygdala is **the brain region that processes emotions**, especially fear and anxiety. This region becomes more active during a divorce, increasing emotional responses.

As a result, you are likely to be more sensitive to emotional cues and experiences related to the divorce. That is why you are or likely will be easily triggered.

2. Impact on the Prefrontal Cortex

The prefrontal cortex, at the front of the brain, *is responsible for decision-making and emotional regulation*. During this period, your brain may engage this part more to help control and manage emotional reactions.

This region plays a role in evaluating and interpreting emotional information and generating appropriate emotional responses.

3. Engage the Limbic System

The limbic system, including the hippocampus and amygdala, *is involved in memory formation and emotional processing*.

Emotions related to divorce can activate this region, encoding emotional memories associated with the divorce process. For example, suppose you caught your ex-spouse in bed with someone else, leading to divorce. In that case, you will likely remember and replay the scenario for a long time.

4. Impact on the Reward and Pleasure Centres

Divorce can disrupt the brain's reward and pleasure centres, such as the mesolimbic dopamine system. This system is involved in experiencing pleasure, motivation, and reward.

Divorce-related stress and emotional turmoil can affect the release and reception of neurotransmitters like dopamine, potentially contributing to feelings of sadness, decreased motivation, and anhedonia (reduced ability to experience pleasure).

5. Impact Social Perception and Mirror Neurons

Mirror neurons in the parietal and premotor cortex **help with empathy and social perception**. They allow you to understand and resonate with others' emotional experiences. This is why you might wonder and worry about how the divorce emotionally impacts other people, especially your kids.

During a divorce, the brain's mirror neuron system may also influence how you perceive and empathise with your emotions. For example, you might hate yourself for breaking your family, whether you initiated the divorce or not.

Knowing how the divorce has or will impact you emotionally and psychologically, let's discuss how you may react.

PEOPLE REACT TO DIVORCE DIFFERENTLY

We all have different personalities with individual emotional responses, coping mechanisms, and traits. As such, everybody processes and navigates through a divorce and its aftermath differently.

Yes, everyone is complex in their way, but here are some ways in which different people are likely to react to a divorce:

1. Analytical Thinkers

If you are an analytical thinker, you will approach the divorce by analysing the situation from all perspectives and aiming for logical solutions. If you are the one who initiated the divorce, you probably thought things through before making the decision, and if not, when your ex-partner served you with divorce papers, one of your first thoughts was perhaps, "What am I going to do? How will I get the finances to pay legal fees or raise the kids? Where am I going to get the best divorce lawyer?"

You use your problem-solving and logical mindset to:

- ***Do thorough research***: Before the legal process began, you probably researched your rights and the divorce procedures. You might have started reading divorce books and articles and reached out to a legal professional to understand the financial and legal implications of the divorce.
- ***Make objective decisions***: You weigh different options, consider all the consequences in every situation, and evaluate the pros and cons before making decisions. You will be across legal procedures such as property division, parenting arrangements, and other divorce settlement aspects to ensure a favourable outcome.
- ***Get the necessary documentation***: You didn't start being an analytical thinker after the divorce. You have been one all your life, and you've probably kept the required documentation safe. So, whether you initiated the divorce or not, you probably have paperwork or spreadsheets for financial assets and other relevant information. This will be useful during your separation and divorce process.
- ***Plan for the future***: Even as you grieve, you will still plan. You will consider how the divorce impacts your finances, personal goals, and career. For example, you might start budgeting or looking for ways to advance your career and explore different ways to rebuild your life.
- ***Seek professional help***: You understand the importance of experts during a divorce, so you probably have sought advice and guidance from counsellors, mediators, financial advisors, or divorce lawyers.

If you are an analytical thinker, you will likely neglect your emotional well-being, which is unhealthy. Ensure that you are making informed decisions on your emotional health too.

2. Resilient Individuals

Resilient individuals tend to possess adaptability and inner strength, which can influence how they navigate the challenges of divorce.

If you are a resilient person, here is how you are likely to react to the divorce:

- *Acceptance and emotional regulation*: The divorce has changed your life, but you will likely accept reality sooner and acknowledge your emotions without becoming overwhelmed. You will experience, or already are experiencing, different emotions, such as anger, confusion, and sadness, but will manage, or are managing, them effectively, allowing you to move forward quickly.
- *Positive outlook and growth mindset*: Even though you face adversity, you probably have decided to view your divorce as an opportunity for positive change and personal growth. You focus on what you can control, like your responses and actions, and strive to build a better future for yourself and your kids.
- *Seeking support and building a support network*: You may contact close friends, family members, or support groups for emotional support and guidance. You are also open to seeking professional help, such as therapy or counselling, to aid you in navigating the emotional and practical challenges of divorce.
- *Self-care and self-reflection*: You understand the importance of taking care of your well-being, so you prioritise self-care activities such as exercise, healthy eating, and engaging in hobbies or activities that bring you joy. You may also self-reflect or engage

in introspection and personal development to better understand yourself and your needs.
- ***Building a new identity and future***: You might view divorce as an opportunity for personal reinvention and creating a new chapter in your life. You focus on building a positive and fulfilling future for yourself, embracing new possibilities and opportunities. You may explore new interests, pursue career goals, or develop new friendships and relationships.

3. Emotional Individuals

Those who are emotionally sensitive might experience intense emotional reactions to divorce. If you are emotional, you may feel a profound sense of betrayal, loss, sadness, and anger. Processing these emotions may take time, and you might find yourself revisiting and reliving the emotional experience long after the legal divorce processes are over, meaning you might grieve for a long time. You find comfort in sharing your experience with friends and family and getting validation, meaning you could benefit from counselling or therapy.

You might find expression and solace through creative activities such as art, music, and writing, which are therapeutic and can help you process your feelings, emotions, and experience. You can find healing through self-care and introspection practices such as meditation and journaling, as they provide insight toward self-growth.

4. Problem Solvers

When you realised you were getting divorced, you might have viewed it as a challenge you needed to overcome. Even though you and your ex-spouse are going in different ways, you still value and understand the importance of effective communication. As such, you won't look to create more trouble or cause drama during legal processes. You may have looked for negotiators or conflict resolution professionals to help make the process peaceful.

You will also likely actively seek solutions, plan, and take practical steps to resolve finance, property, and parenting issues.

5. Avoidant Individuals

If you have an avoidant personality style, it may affect how you respond to divorce in the following ways:

- ***Emotional detachment***: If you have this personality, you may detach yourself emotionally from the divorce process as a coping mechanism. In other words, you may not want anything to do with the divorce, either legally or personally. Also, you may suppress or minimise your feelings to avoid facing the sadness, pain, or anger associated with the end of the relationship. This emotional distancing can be your way of self-preservation.
- ***Avoiding conflict***: You may try to avoid conflict and go to great lengths to avoid confrontations during divorce proceedings. You may opt for mediation or collaborative processes instead of litigation. To avoid making things escalate and maintain peace, you may compromise more than necessary, even at the expense of your needs.
- ***Withdrawing from discussions***: You may withdraw from decision-making processes or talks related to the divorce. You might even leave the majority of negotiations to your former spouse or legal professionals. This withdrawal can be a way of protecting yourself from potential emotional discomfort or disagreement.
- ***Seeking distraction***: You may engage in distracting activities such as hobbies, social engagements, or work to avoid dealing

with the emotional pain of the divorce. You may even revert to substance abuse, alcohol consumption, or meaningless sex to temporarily escape the situation's realities and emotional impact.
- ***Difficulty seeking support***: You may struggle to seek or accept emotional support from others as you find it challenging to open up about your feelings or vulnerabilities.
- ***Internalising blame***: You may internalise accountability or responsibility for the divorce, even if it was a mutual decision or due to circumstances beyond your control. You might take on self-criticism and excessive guilt, which can further hinder your ability to process your emotions effectively.

6. People Pleasers

Being a people pleaser means you have a strong desire to please others and may struggle with divorce due to feelings of shame and guilt or fear of disappointing others. As such, you may experience anxiety and fear of judgement and disapproval, have difficulties asserting your perspective and seeking help, and experience emotional distress in cases of conflict. You may put other people's needs, your ex-partner's and your kids', before yours and, as such, may compromise a lot and have difficulty setting boundaries and moving on.

What About Your Ex?

Dealing with a divorce is overwhelming, especially if your ex-partner is difficult. You know where you belong, which can significantly help your divorce journey. But do you know your ex-spouse's personality? Do they like playing games, scheming, plotting, and treating you like the enemy? Did family violence, whether coercive control, psychological, or physical, lead to your divorce? In addition to psychological issues, is physical safety also relevant? All or some of these factors can significantly impact the divorce process.

In Chapter 5, we will discuss in detail some of the games people going through divorce play and the strategies they use, and we will look at how to deal with them so that your mental, physical, and emotional health doesn't suffer.

It's important to remember that ***two types of difficult spouses generally exist***. Your ex-partner might be difficult now as a way of reacting to the divorce, but once they process the divorce and come to terms with everything, they are likely to move on with their life. On the other hand, the permanently difficult ex is likely to make your life difficult regardless of the outcome, and that is why later, you will learn ways to deal with them and create a plan for yourself and your children.

But for now, let's move on to the next section and learn how divorce impacts kids and how you can co-parent and make adjustments to help make the divorce experience less challenging for them.

Chapter 2:

Your Kids Come First

Navigating through a divorce is a journey. The experience you go through during a divorce will shape your life in terms of parenting, finances, and health. Your attitude towards each other, your ability to be patient, and how well you and your ex can cooperate will determine whether the transition will be easy or difficult.

If you have children, you both must put aside your differences and consider how the divorce has affected or will affect them emotionally, psychologically, financially, and even physically. Don't say, *"They are kids, and they will just get over it,"* because divorce affects all the parties involved, including your kids. How you act, talk, or react to your children and your ex-spouse concerning the separation might impact how your child will turn out now and in the future. If you put your children in the middle of everything and use them as messengers to communicate with your ex, they will be caught up in the drama and likely blame themselves for whatever happened.

Remember this: you are responsible for your child's well-being, and no matter how ugly things get during the divorce, their happiness and stability should be at the front of your mind.

So moving forward, you and your ex must develop a new mindset and learn how to compromise as you navigate and embrace your new way of life. As such, having profound knowledge of divorce's pitfalls or potential effects on your kids is essential as it will enable you and your ex to implement measures to suppress adverse effects.

This section will discuss the impact of divorce and conflict on your children and how to develop a co-parenting plan as you adapt to the new norm.

IMPACT OF DIVORCE AND CONFLICT ON CHILDREN

Every day is a learning day, especially for children. Your children will look up to you and your ex for guidance. If you display unhealthy behaviours in front of them, such as arguing and fighting or negatively talking about the other parent, they will pick up these cues.

Children respond differently to divorce depending on their age and stage of development and other considerations, including whether they have special needs or ongoing medical requirements. Ultimately, most children are resilient; all they need is for you to implement strategic methods to deal appropriately with the changes that come with divorce, live close together, and communicate well with your ex. Easy … right?!

But, seriously, the better your separation and divorce are managed, the better your children will cope with the inevitable change when one household becomes two.

Before we move on, there are some important things to note. **There is no one-size-fits-all answer to parenting arrangements**. The conflict that each family experiences is different.

Some families experience extreme conflict, including family and domestic violence, with physical injuries or psychological manipulation. Other families deal with mental health issues, including depression and anxiety, and sometimes there are untreated, severe or undiagnosed mental health issues, including personality disorders. Families also experience issues with drug and alcohol misuse. Some families experience all of these issues at the same time.

It may be that in your family, it is not possible to communicate effectively or work through a parenting plan because of these issues. Safety planning may be a priority, and protecting your children from exposure to a parent with serious substance misuse issues may be your priority. You will still pick up some key points on the following pages, but *it is important that you consider the concepts in the context of your own circumstances.*

Types of Conflicts During a Divorce

Every divorce is different, as are the types of conflicts people can experience. How you and your ex handle every aspect of your divorce will determine how your children will be affected.

Here are some common divorce disagreements and their impact on your children:

1. High-conflict Divorce

Do you feel like you and your ex lack cooperation? Are you constantly engaging in never-ending disagreements accompanied by hostility and frequent arguments? Does it feel like you are fighting about everything? You may even have added issues relating to family and domestic violence or psychological or safety concerns in the mix.

If so, your children are caught up in a high-conflict divorce, and what you might forget during this period when everything seems to be falling apart is that **children are great observers**. During a heated argument between you and your ex, your children listen to the commotion and conversations, and sometimes, they might be unfortunate and watch the nightmare happen right before their eyes.

Your children may question their relationships with each of you, particularly if the conflict is manipulative or covert. Your children might "pick sides", leading to emotional turmoil and increasing conflicts, worsening things. When children pick sides, it is hard to convince them otherwise since they have lost your trust. They see the parent they don't choose the side of as an enemy, an outsider who doesn't want the best for them.

Such experiences can lead to chronic stress, anxiety, and depression.

Additionally, your children may become emotionally unstable when they witness you and your ex getting the better of each other in heated arguments or physical or verbal violence. For example, they might think you don't love them if they hear you arguing about childcare.

These behaviours can manifest in children later in life and impact their mental health and their ability to form relationships with others. It impacts a child's ability to trust and how they cope when faced with adversity. Children who experience high-conflict divorce may misuse drugs and alcohol to cope with difficulties that arise in adulthood.

2. Conflict About Legal Proceedings

"See you in court!" A simple phrase that carries enormous weight for the individual who has to bear the consequences if unprepared. During the divorce, you might have to settle things such as parenting arrangements, childcare, and other financial matters. Court procedures take a long time before the final decision is delivered and are accompanied by scheduled travels to the courtroom and meetings with your lawyer to prepare the case.

While some court processes might be necessary to sanction agreements or have a court determine an outcome where parties cannot agree, court processes can also be used as a weapon to control the other party, put up barriers, and make day-to-day life difficult. Going to court and having a lawyer costs money. If you can't afford legal representation, you might find a nasty party on the other side using that to their advantage.

During this lengthy period of up and down legal proceedings, as much as you try to protect your children from the process, home life will be stressful and uncertain for them. The court proceedings can get heated, and you and your ex may argue in the presence of your children and undergo intense evaluations, contributing to feelings of insecurity and anxiety. Your children will see their home matters being discussed openly as you all try to determine their fate. Amid the confusion and conflict between you and your ex, your children will build their own version of the facts, true or not, which can significantly affect their emotional and psychological well-being.

3. Financial Conflicts

Divorce has financial implications for you, your ex, and your children. A household surviving on two incomes is now pivoting to move forward on one income. It is a complex reality to live by, and this can affect how you react to financial matters, leading to disputes over child support, alimony and maintenance, property division, or financial responsibilities. When you and your spouse disagree about dividing your assets and how you will settle shared bills, your children might suffer. The parent paying child support might want to "punish" the other by fighting in court to get a favourable deal where they contribute the least amount possible. This will likely directly affect your children, who might miss out on necessities.

Financial constraints lower a family's standard of living due to reduced cash flow to purchase essential goods and services for the children. As a result, your children may experience financial instability and reduced access to resources and opportunities.

4. Emotional Conflict

Emotional conflicts involve intense reactions and unresolved anger, grief, or resentment between you and your ex. A divorce situation where you or your ex go back and forth in blaming one another for the untimely end of a marriage is a cause for emotional conflict. You will feel resentment and seek validation or emotional support from your children. As a parent, you need to be strong and take on any adversity. Still, your children can develop emotional distress if you depend on them to provide emotional security and stability.

When you struggle to manage your emotions during divorce, your children may witness outbursts, conflicts, and hostile interactions. Children in emotional conflict keep to themselves and barely let themselves interact with their peers. The events and happenings during and after divorce are complex for them, making it difficult to contain and regulate their feelings, negatively impacting their self-esteem and overall emotional development. Children are naturally playful, but children exposed to the emotional stress of divorce can be withdrawn and unmotivated due to instability at home.

5. Conflict About Parenting Arrangements

Regardless of the outcome of your separation and divorce, you and your ex will continue to be the parents of your children. Parenting conflict occurs when you and your ex have ongoing disagreements about parenting styles, decision-making, or implementation of parenting arrangements. For example, disagreeing on how you will structure the arrangements for children is a source of conflict.

One of you might feel disadvantaged and undoubtedly express your grievances, which, if not addressed, starts the blame game. When you struggle to communicate effectively and cooperate as parents, your children may experience inconsistency and conflicting expectations. They don't know who to turn to when they are looking for someone to cater to their needs, leading to emotional and behavioural difficulties. Your children may also feel caught up in loyalty conflicts, especially if they witness parents speaking negatively about the other parent.

6. Conflicts About Where Parties Live

After a divorce or during the separation process, it is inevitable that one parent will need to leave the family home. Conflicts will occur where there is a disagreement about which parent leaves, followed by ongoing discussions about how the children will spend time with each of the parents.

Your children will face the challenge of adjusting to a new environment, such as changing schools and separation from friends and extended family. These changes can also disorient and disrupt the support systems you put in place before the divorce, such as play dates, negatively impacting the social and emotional being of a child as a consequence.

It is important to note that children react to divorce conflicts differently. Some may experience immediate distress, while others may show resilience in adversity. However, prolonged exposure to extreme levels of hostility is ultimately detrimental to children and can leave them with lasting and ongoing behavioural issues into the future.

Children can experience the following:

- A sense of abandonment and insecurity where a parent leaves with no or little ongoing relationship
- Poor academic performance due to confusion and distraction, leading to disengagement from their education
- A likelihood of risk-taking behaviour, pushing the boundaries, being in trouble with the law, and indulging in substance and alcohol use
- Ongoing emotional dysregulation

Children from divorced homes, particularly where they are exposed to conflict, have a higher rate of ***general mental health dysfunction*** regardless of age, gender, race, and cultural background. The psychological phenomenon in kids affected by divorce may manifest in depression, delinquency, and impulsive behaviour.

During the early stages of divorce, you will observe a shift in behaviour, such as unnecessary recurrent conflict among peers. You will also notice a change in their emotions, ranging from sadness, confusion, anger, and guilt to fear. Fear cultivates a sense of insecurity in your children, making them weary and anxious about the future regarding the changes that divorce brings in their lives. Your child might feel ashamed that you and your ex are separated, yet their friends' parents are still together, significantly impacting their self-esteem.

All of these factors must be at the front of your mind when you decide how to behave during and manage your divorce process. These are choices you must make.

Are there any positive impacts of divorce on children? If there are, they are limited.

Divorce will ultimately change the way you manage your life. Where work was a priority for you or your ex during your relationship, you are now **making more time to be available for your children**, spending time with them and working on your relationship.

The most significant positive impact for children is **reducing conflict in a marriage that was not working**. A chaotic environment is a time bomb waiting to explode, and your kids are in the middle of the crossfire. Before the divorce, you might have noticed that your children would rather have stayed at their friend's place if you often fought with your ex. And if this was the situation in your marriage, divorce can be a lifesaver and peacemaker as it reduces tension and stress.

Children are susceptible to feeling their parents' emotions, which can trigger episodes of anxiety and stress if exposed to too much conflict at home. On the other hand, if the hostile environment doesn't exist, the exposure to adverse consequences reduces.

How Do Kids Cope With or React to the New Norm?

It's a no-brainer that every divorce is different, and so are the reactions your children display in a bid to deal with the alien norm that seeks to tear apart their families. The mechanism children use to cope with change varies depending on their age, temperament, and previous experiences. Understanding how your children will react to your divorce will allow you to assist them in coping with this new norm.

Emotions run high during a divorce for both parents and children. ***The uncertainty and confusion cause the build-up of emotions such as sadness, anger, fear, and anxiety.*** Your child might become more clingy and irritable and showcase regressive behaviours such as bedwetting or thumb-sucking.

Change is challenging, even for your children. At this point, they feel a range of emotions, making them resist or express opposition to change. Their *resistance is a way for them to maintain control and familiarity*, and they might be reluctant to try new things or become upset with the changes in their routines.

You and your ex are busy dealing with your fair share of divorce challenges, which might lead you to forget how the situation impacts your children or assume they are too young to notice or be affected. However, they will notice your absence or your ex's, which will cause them to feel neglected. As such, *your children may seek reassurance from trusted adults* such as other parents, teachers, or caregivers.

Change can affect a child's behaviour, and you might sometimes be concerned by the new range of reactions. Some kids may display heightened excitement or energy as a response to change. In contrast, others might exhibit increased defiance, become more withdrawn, or have difficulty concentrating, characterised by daydreaming or being lost in deep thoughts.

Observe the behaviour patterns of your kids closely. Watch out for your toddlers and preschoolers since regression and tantrums can affect them as they deal with and cope with divorce. **You might notice your children reverting to behaviours they had previously outgrown**, such as wanting a pacifier, using baby talk, or having trouble with toilet training.

Play is essential for children to process and make sense of the world by interacting with their peers. Your children might incorporate themes related to the change into their imaginative play or use toys to act out scenarios and express their feelings.

While your children react to change with various emotions and behaviours, they possess remarkable resilience and adaptability. As time goes by, ***given the necessary support they need and the opportunity to adjust***, many children gradually become comfortable and resilient to change. Soon, your kid will become more cheerful, friendly, and energetic, and you will wonder if they were ever going through difficult times.

What You Can Do to Help Your Kids Cope With Change

How you manage the situation will determine how your children cope with and react to change. Doing away with the way things have always been and the norms of the past relationship can be complex for kids, but with your intervention, they will flourish.

Here are things you can initiate to help your kids better deal with the new norm from now on.

You should **maintain open and honest communication** between your ex and the children. Constantly reassure the children that you love them dearly and that the divorce is not their fault to alleviate anxiety. Let them know that you both will always be there for them, so they should not be afraid to open up and express their feelings and needs to either of you.

When parents explain divorce clearly and consistently offer emotional support, children are more likely to understand and adapt to the changes.

Maintaining stability is essential to make your children feel secure during a change. During a divorce, you and your ex have conflicts that might prevent the two of you from engaging the children in meaningful routines.

However, you both should put on brave faces and indicate that you are still in charge despite the internal struggles. It would be best if you worked together to establish consistent routines for your children, including consistent schedules for visitation, meals, and bedtime.

Predictability and structure provide a sense of normalcy that supports children's adjustments.

Co-parenting is a joint parenting undertaking in which the parents work in unison to raise their children, creating a positive environment. *Cooperating and collaborating in raising your children after a divorce fosters a sense of belonging and love* for a family in the children. Additionally, it reduces stress and uncertainty for all.

You and your ex both have responsibility for your children's behaviours. Some things you and your ex can **role model** and practise for your children's sake are demonstrating healthy coping strategies, maintaining positive relationships, and embracing new routines, which can set an excellent example for the children. Ensuring you always talk about the other parent respectfully and positively is also important.

Being resilient and adaptable can positively impact how your children cope with change. When your children see you and your ex-spouse constructively navigating and adapting to change, they are more likely to develop similar skills.

As you've noticed so far, divorce is a rollercoaster for both the parents and the children. Your children may experience various emotions following the divorce, including sadness, anger, confusion, and fear. As a parent, you should be able to **detect the emotional effects on your child** and prepare amicable solutions to make them feel appreciated. For example, you and your ex should talk through your children's emotions and feelings and be there for them by encouraging them to open up. Commit to assuring your children that they are safe, their feelings are okay, and they can turn to you.

It is vital to note that with even the best efforts from parents, children may still experience various challenges and emotions during and after a divorce. In such cases, seeking professional support, such as therapy or counselling, can be beneficial for your children to process their feelings and develop effective coping strategies. Various other risk factors may be at play that can hinder a child's progress in a divorce, such as mental health, drugs, alcohol misuse, and family violence. If so, seek help from experts with experience in helping children cope.

COMING UP WITH A PLAN FOR YOUR KIDS MOVING FORWARD

How nice would it be if we had a crystal ball to gaze into and work out the following steps: where each parent will be living, how the children will manage the new living arrangements, and how everyone, parents included, is coping with the divorce? It would be wonderful, but it isn't an option, unfortunately.

The best way to manage the new normal is to think about the time frames for the next point and plan for that. *Having a short-term, mid-term, and long-term plan is sometimes the best you can do*.

A *short-term plan* may involve the time from separation to the new living arrangements. Who is moving out of the house (if someone is moving out), where will they stay, and how can they spend time with the children? How old are the children – a newborn or very young child will benefit from short, frequent time with the other parent to grow and maintain a bond; older children may already have stronger attachments to both parents, so they will be able to cope with a few days away from the other parent without impacting that bond.

A ***mid-term plan*** may be required when parents are in separate but temporary houses and the divorce settlement has yet to be finalised. A parent may be waiting on the outcome of an agreed sale or a hearing to know where they will be able to set up a new home. A mid-term plan allows for some flexibility, knowing that this is the "for now" plan, and once the parents ultimately settle all aspects of their divorce, there will be more stability. Similar factors about the children's ages and stages of development are also relevant here.

The length of time a ***long-term plan*** needs to be in place will depend largely on the ages of the children. It is difficult to plan with any certainty what parenting arrangements for children who are three, four, or five years of age will look like when they are 12. There is attendance at school to factor in. As they get older, children might spend more time with the other parent; they may transition to spending equal time with both parents. A parent may be unable to afford to live in the same area, which may impact the long-term plan.

In addition to thinking about whether it is a short-term, mid-term, or long-term plan, it is essential to think about the following.

All children are different, just like adults. It is important not to generalise the arrangements but to **consider the individual needs of your children**. Each child is unique and has a different makeup in terms of weaknesses, strengths, and interests. Fashion your strategies and plans to accommodate their individuality regarding age, personality, and abilities. Remember to **keep in mind any special or medical needs** of your children and how those needs will be managed across two households.

Prioritise the education of your children. We live in a competitive world where a slight advantage can give you an edge in a fast-moving world spearheaded by technology. Therefore, education is a fundamental element necessary for the development of children.

Start by establishing a new routine for handling homework and providing educational materials or any training they may require to expand their knowledge. Encourage and motivate them to study as much as possible to help shape their future. It is particularly important to know how conflict impacts your children and the impact that conflict has on their learning potential. Stability and routine are essential to give your children the best opportunity to move forward.

In your parenting plan, include strategies to support their academic progress. Be actively involved in their schooling activities by following up and showing up on occasions requiring your presence.

Encourage your children to pursue their interests and passions. Provide the resources and cultivate environments that give them opportunities to explore various activities, hobbies, and subjects. Their talents might be in sports, arts, sciences, or other areas. Within your plans moving forward, identify ways to help them develop their skills and talents.

Take time off work's busy schedule and ***spend time with your children to understand them more.*** Previously, your work routine may have meant you were less available for your children. Take time away from work to help your children settle into new routines and homes. Pay attention to your children's emotions and encourage open communication, active listening, and empathy within the family. Talk to your children and **teach them emotional intelligence** so they can recognise and manage their emotions effectively. Create a supportive and positive environment where your children feel safe expressing themselves and seeking guidance when needed.

Co-parenting

Co-parenting is *the collective effort put in by both parents to raise their children despite having separated or undergoing a divorce*. Since it's a new concept on the block, parents find it hard to co-parent, often feeling as though they are doing the work and that the other parent "gets all the fun time" or they are "losing time" with the children. Despite your differences, you must find approaches that suit your children's needs.

Remember, co-parenting is not about competing with one another on who the child will love most. The last thing your child needs is a stressful scenario brought about by competitive parenting. During divorce is not the time to get back at your ex by talking to the children about their shortcomings.

Before we get into the details you need to include in your parenting plan, keep these things in mind to ensure that you give your family the best possibility of moving forward.

Formulate a detailed plan on how you will handle your children's needs. Who takes care of what? A plan gives you a road map and a direction to follow so that conflict of interest doesn't arise, derailing the whole endeavour. Each parent's role is distinct but often overlaps, so you must be flexible and not feel overworked.

Depending on your children's needs, including their ages and stages of development, *think about what arrangements work best for your family*. Younger children might need to spend more time with the primary parent and regular time with the other parent. Older children will be able to spend more time away from their primary parent. Think about the health and medical needs of your children. Also, think about the practicalities for each parent – does one parent work shift work, is one away for work a lot, are both parents available and local to work together?

Minimise conflict in the presence of the children. Respect yourself and your ex and develop a habit of discussing issues instead of having heated arguments. Also, distance your children from the court proceedings, which can be daunting and difficult for them to wrap their heads around.

Take time to **explain to your children the new norm of life** so that it doesn't come as a shock, leaving them in confusion. You and your ex must take responsibility and be open with your children. If you can come up with a plan to talk to your children together and support each other in joint messaging, then your children will adapt more quickly. You don't want a young detective unearthing misconduct as that will make the child resentful toward you or your ex.

Divorce is difficult for all parties involved, and its impact can have a long-term effect on a child. Remember, you have to be super conscious of your own behaviour for your own sake, as well as the collective well-being of your children. If you find it challenging to co-parent peacefully, seek expert help from a therapist with experience in dealing with divorce families.

Creating a Co-parenting Plan

You should prepare a parenting plan to enable you and your ex to move forward. The procedure can be a formal, detailed legal document or a verbal agreement regarding your children's parenting affairs.

The plan should detail how your kids spend time with you and your ex and how you will make decisions and avoid conflict. The specific details of your parenting plan will depend on where you live and the law that applies to your jurisdiction. Generally, you should consider the following to guide you in creating a parenting plan.

If you have young children yet to start formal schooling, think about how you will manage the day-to-day. Are the children going to daycare or being breastfed? Remember that very young children will benefit from ensuring their attachment to their primary parent remains secure. At the same time, children should spend regular short visits with the other parent to build and maintain a bond.

When children are at school age, think about the following groups of time:

- School week time
- School weekends
- School holidays or vacation time
- Special holidays, long weekends, and other special occasions

During the school week, stability and routine are crucial. Remember, the impact of conflict on children will impact their schooling if that process is not managed well. Follow homework and study routines. Try to have this happen across both households and reach an agreement with your ex about this.

Weekends are usually full of activities, sporting events, extracurricular activities, birthday parties, and play dates. Who will take the children to these events? Both parents need to be on the same page here; if one parent decides that they are not going to be involved in those activities during "my weekend", the children, and only the children, miss out. A way to avoid arguments here is to ensure you are both on the same page about the activities the children will attend.

Think about how you will manage *school holiday time*. Holidays vary worldwide, but generally, there are short-break holidays and longer year-end holidays. How old are the children? Should time be shared in shorter visits? Is a long block period appropriate? Do you have plans to travel to see family or to go overseas? Think about fairness here so that the children spend a reasonable amount of time with each parent, and if the time is uneven, make sure you swap the following year.

Mixed up in those holidays are special days. ***Christmas and other significant holidays*** are always difficult to navigate. Some things to think about are these:

- If you live close to each other, think about whether time can be shared on Christmas Day and other days of significance.
- For young children, it is important for them to see both parents on the day if this is possible.
- If the distance between homes means it will take more than about 30 mins to changeover, think about whether it is practical to share the day. Whilst the parents might have some joy in the time, it is the children who will need to spend time in the car on the day.
- Consider alternating special holidays so the children can be in one place and enjoy the day.

Depending on the relationship between you and your ex, you may decide to have a family get-together, keeping any differences aside and focusing on creating memorable experiences for your children instead of images of a dysfunctional family. Those families only seem to appear in the movies, so you need to determine what works for you. Children will pick up on awkward behaviour if there is too much tension.

Think about how you will manage ***other special days*** – birthdays for children and parents, Mother's Day and Father's Day, and any other significant days for your family. Is it practical to share time on the day? Will a video call be sufficient?

Do you need to set aside a specific time for when phone calls happen or how you will communicate with each other?

Regularly review your parenting plan to determine any changes that might be necessary. The changes might be temporary or permanent, depending on the dynamics. You might need a plan right now because there are a lot of unknowns at the moment, or you are parenting an infant. You may need a short-term co-parenting plan because your child is becoming an adult soon and will be able to support themselves.

Consult with your ex and **establish who will make certain daily decisions on essential matters**. Depending on your preferences, you can choose one of you, both of you, or the parent with whom the children live primarily as the immediate decision-maker. Either way, make sure the decision considers the children's needs and the other parent's views, and if the decision is essential or impacts the children spending time with the other parent, that communication is clear.

Think about any **medical or health requirements for your children**. How will you manage appointments? Will you both attend? And how will you keep each other in the loop about what is happening? Also, **think about how you will pay for essential things for your children** – are the children attending a private school, or are you paying for additional tuition? Are their costs associated with their health care management – how will you manage those costs? If you agree about these things, you will remove a lot of future conflict from the equation.

It will be important to **consider your living arrangements now and in the future** (as best you can without that crystal ball). Where will you both live in the short term? Will that impact how the children will spend time with each of you? If one parent moves away, what do new arrangements look like with distance and travel involved? How will you accommodate and pay for the travel?

The specifics involved in a parenting plan may vary depending on the circumstances at play with your children's needs and what you would love to see as parents moving forward. If you are stuck on any of the points above, you should talk to a family therapist for advice about what might work well for the children or a mediator to have an independent person facilitate discussion and come up with ideas that might work. You should also consult your lawyer for advice about managing and documenting this process.

Before we finish this chapter about your children, there are a few more terms that you may have heard of when it comes to thinking about what parenting arrangements might work. Sometimes people get hung up on these terms, so it is important to know that the label you apply to your parenting plan doesn't really matter – so long as the children are settled and spending appropriate time with each parent.

Parallel parenting is an arrangement that is said to work best in a conflict situation where interactions and communication between you and your ex are a no-go zone. One parent will manage their household how they wish, and the other parent will manage their household how they wish. Both parents have little regard for what the other parent does. There is no communication or consistency. The level of hatred is usually pretty high, and you generally have little regard for the other parent.

Cooperative parenting is different from parallel parenting in that you work together in unison to make appropriate decisions regarding the upbringing and overall well-being of your children. Communication between you and your ex is maintained as you strive to initiate consistent parenting styles and routines. The overall aim is to establish and foster a positive co-parenting relationship. This is the gold star of parenting post-divorce.

Bird's nest parenting involves you and your ex taking turns living with the children, who stay in one home. Instead of the children moving between two houses, the parents alternate living with them.

Picture a bird's nest where both birds take turns visiting the nest to take note of their young ones by feeding them or keeping them company. The same routine is possible in humans since it provides stability for the children. However, there must be constant communication between you two.

Whilst it might seem ideal for the children, it is not so for the parents who remain stuck in the separation cycle, unable to move forward. In my experience, I have seen this work well on two occasions – one for a short period where the parents were separated but still living together. Both parents gradually started to spend time away from home for a couple of nights at a time, allowing the children to have one-on-one time with the other parent. The other occasion was also short-term, but there were six children, and it was impossible for either parent to house the children separately in two households.

A *week-about or alternating weeks parenting arrangement* might work for your family. Here, the children are moving from one home to another, spending one week with you and another week with your ex. This method provides equal opportunity for the children to spend time with you and your ex. It works best if you have good communication, you live close to each other and the children's school, and the children are older (at least school age) and have formed strong bonds with both parents, enabling them to be away from their primary carer for up to seven days at a time.

The week-about or equal-time arrangement can be split in a number of ways across a two-week block if your children are too young to spend seven days at a time with each parent – so long as the arrangement is consistent and there is not too much back and forward for the children.

CO-PARENTING WITH A DIFFICULT EX

What if your ex is difficult to deal with? We often hear the word "narcissist" used in family law and divorce, particularly when dealing with difficult people. Often these people won't let reason prevail, no matter how hard you try.

Here is how to go about *co-parenting with a difficult (or narcissistic) parent*.

Co-parenting with a difficult parent can be challenging and emotionally draining. If your ex is a narcissist, they are probably overly possessive because they see your child as an extension of themselves. They bully you and take control as the sole decision-maker, guiding the children's lives by controlling their every move.

Some tips that can help you navigate the situation to minimise the impact on your children as you deal with a narcissistic parent in co-parenting include the following.

Establish clear boundaries with the other parent to foster a healthy relationship. Take time and clearly define expectations, responsibilities, and limits to ensure your children are doing fine as you protect yourself from manipulation or emotional abuse.

Strictly focus on the children and have their best interests at heart. Every decision you make should reference the safety and happiness of the children rather than getting entangled with power struggles with the narcissistic parent.

Document all the communication and interactions you have with the other parent. It may come in handy in case a legal battle ensues since it will be concrete evidence of the behaviour patterns of the parent.

Don't wait until things get out of hand; **consider seeking professional help**. Therapists, mediators, or counsellors are your best bet for guidance and support as you navigate co-parenting with a difficult parent.

The professionals will help you develop effective strategies to cope with the challenges of protecting your children.

Foster healthy communication and maintain a business-like profile by not saying more than you should. Avoid arguments; they will get you emotionally drawn into their manipulation circus. Discuss matters relating to children only, period.

Co-parenting with a difficult (or narcissistic) parent is stressful and can drain your emotional energy. So, ***take care of your mind, body, and spirit*** as you dwell on self-care activities. Consider professional therapy.

There is a lot to consider in this chapter about looking after your children. Take the time to consider carefully the possible outcomes if the process is not managed well. How you choose to manage your parenting relationship, communicate, and co-parent with your ex will ultimately set your children up to survive the divorce process.

Chapter 3:

Managing Your Money

Everybody gets married hoping to make it a lifetime commitment, and so you probably thought that you would forever have your spouse to work together with to figure out and manage most, if not all, of the finances. But, unfortunately, this is not the case, and whether you initiated the divorce or not, these thoughts have probably crossed your mind:

How will I pay the bills on my own without stretching my pockets?
How will I be able to save for my future and that of my kids?
How can I make more money to sustain my lifestyle?
I need a new budget; how do I develop one?

Welcome to Chapter 3, where we delve into managing your money during the challenging divorce process. Yes, the transition during divorce is difficult, but no matter how hard it is on you, you must make an effort to understand how to navigate your financial landscape for a smooth and secure future.

One thing is for sure – managing your finances during divorce requires careful planning, a clear understanding of your assets and debts, and the ability to make informed decisions. During this time, your emotions might impair your judgments, causing you to act carelessly and make financial decisions that may negatively impact your life. However, by taking a practical approach and arming yourself with knowledge, you can gain the confidence to make sound financial choices that will see you have control of your post-divorce life.

This section will explore practical considerations, strategies, and insights to help you effectively manage your finances during this period. It will guide you through the various aspects of handling your money throughout the divorce process. We will start by helping you assess your assets and gather the necessary documents to interpret your financial situation. Then, we'll explore the significance of creating a budget that reflects your new reality, considering both the current household and the potential changes with two separate households.

You will also learn the practical strategies for managing day-to-day expenses and gain insights into understanding legal fees, which can often be a concern during divorce proceedings. Moreover, we will discuss how you can consider a collaborative mindset when approaching financial matters, understanding all parties' needs.

Lastly, we'll highlight the importance of avoiding financial mistakes during this critical time. Divorce can magnify the consequences of errors, so seeking professional advice and making thoughtful decisions are paramount to safeguarding your economic well-being.

You might think there is no way out of your financial situation, and your life will worsen. However, by empowering yourself with knowledge, carefully planning your money, and using a collaborative approach, you can confidently navigate the financial aspects of divorce.

So, let's dive into the details of managing your money and equip you with the tools necessary to make informed decisions that will shape your financial future.

ASSESSING YOUR FINANCIAL CIRCUMSTANCES

Before you decide anything, your first step should be understanding your assets and debts. This step is necessary because it will help you make informed decisions regarding the division and allocation of your money, allowing you to develop a suitable plan moving forward.

Know Your Assets and Debts

Here are the steps to follow when trying to understand your financial position.

First, **make a list of all your assets**. This includes collating bank accounts, tax returns, properties (including land, houses, apartments, units, duplexes, etc.), vehicles, investment accounts, valuable possessions, retirement accounts, and other assets with financial value.

Tax returns are papers filed with the tax authorities by businesses or people to account for their expenses, incomes, and other related financial information for a given financial year. These returns are filed annually and record your financial activities as a taxpayer throughout that period. When taking stock of your assets, assessing your tax returns is essential. It will help you understand your overall income from your salary, individual and shared assets, and financial holdings. It will also provide insight into some undisclosed assets or hidden incomes you might not know of. In addition, understanding the tax implications of different assets will help you make informed decisions on which assets you may want to retain, transfer, or sell, now or in the future.

So, take your time to think through and identify all the assets you own. Also, ensure you determine and identify the ownership of property. Did you or your ex own the asset before you met? Is it something that you bought when you were together? Is the asset in your name, your ex's, or in joint names? Rules and laws about assets vary from jurisdiction to jurisdiction, so research or consult a divorce lawyer to help you understand how they apply to you.

The process does not stop there. **You must have the relevant documentation**. Gather your bank statements, vehicle titles, investment account statements, property deeds, appraisals, and other applicable paperwork.

After that, **categorise your assets** to make it simpler for you to review and access the information. For instance, you can organise them as financial accounts, real estate, and personal possessions like artwork and jewellery, etc. Categorising your assets will help you maintain clarity and structure throughout the process.

Capture essential asset details such as current market value and account numbers. This will provide a comprehensive awareness of your assets and their respective financial values. Obtain professional appraisals for current assets such as valuable possessions, businesses, and real estate. They will help you know your asset's current market value precisely, which will help you during negotiations for asset division during the divorce process. If you have partnerships or shared businesses with your ex, consider consulting an accountant or business valuation expert to help you realise the value of the business based on assets, liabilities, market conditions, and financial records.

To make your list more efficient, easily accessible, trackable, and more organised, ***consider utilising digital tools*** such as personal finance software or spreadsheets. However, remember to safeguard your digital documents with passwords and keep your hard copies safe.

For debts, you also must start by ***gathering the necessary documents***. Compile all relevant financial records, including bank statements, credit card statements, loan agreements, mortgage documents, and records of other debts or liabilities.

Go through each financial document and ***determine which debts are joint and which are individual***. Generally, joint debts are those that both spouses are legally responsible for, while personal/individual debts are solely in one spouse's name. Again, remember that rules and laws vary here, and even though a debt is in one person's name, it can be considered in the negotiations.

Review any prenuptial agreements. If you and your spouse have a prenuptial agreement that addresses asset distribution and debt allocation, review it carefully to work out how assets and debts should be shared. These agreements may specify how joint debts should be divided or how individual arrears will be assigned.

Some jurisdictions also refer to community property and

non-community property states. In *a **community property state***, the general rule is that debts incurred during the marriage are considered community debts and may be divided equally between spouses, regardless of whose name is on the debt. On the other hand, ***non-community property states*** follow an equitable distribution principle, where the division of debts is determined based on various factors, including contributions to the debt, earning capacity, and the financial needs of each spouse.

However, ***seek professional advice*** from a divorce lawyer in your jurisdiction. They can guide you on the specific laws in your area and help you understand the potential repercussions of dividing debts differently.

While at it, ***work with your ex-spouse*** and their legal representation to negotiate a fair and mutually agreeable division of joint and individual assets and debts. Consider each spouse's earning potential, financial resources, income, and other relevant circumstances.

It may be beneficial or necessary to ***restructure or refinance debts*** to remove one spouse's name from joint obligations or reduce the overall burden. This may involve working with creditors or lenders to modify or form new loan agreements. If this option works for you, your divorce lawyer will assist you in properly documenting the agreed-upon division in your divorce settlement agreement. This legal document should clearly outline the spouse responsible for each debt and associated repayment terms.

It is essential to note that putting this information together and considering all of these issues can be challenging, especially when your emotional and mental states might not be at their best. Therefore, whenever you get overwhelmed or feel uncertain about any asset or debt, consider consulting with professionals, such as financial planners or family lawyers specialising in divorce. They will provide legal guidance on your assets and debts and ensure you know your obligations and rights during the division process.

Now, let's move on to the next section and learn how to handle all your bills effectively based on your financial circumstances.

CREATE A BUDGET FOR YOUR CURRENT LIVING SITUATION

Now that you know your assets and debts, you can use the knowledge acquired to create a new budget for you and your children. This is essential because a solid budget will help ensure financial stability during and after the divorce. Creating a well-structured budget allows you to regain control of your finances, plan for the future, and make informed decisions that align with your new circumstances.

Here are the essential steps of creating a budget during and after divorce, helping you gain financial independence and peace of mind:

1. Identify Essential and Non-essential Expenses

When creating a budget, it is important to differentiate between essential and non-essential expenses to prioritise your spending effectively.

So, here is how to categorise them:

- ***Basic necessities****:* Start by identifying the expenses necessary to meet your and your children's needs. These typically include rent or mortgage payments, home insurance, property rates and taxes, electricity, heating, water, internet services, grocery bills, essential household supplies, and vehicle-related expenses, such as insurance, fuel, maintenance, and public transportation costs. Consider health insurance premiums, medical bills, prescription medications, and necessary healthcare services.

- *Child-related expenses*: Certain expenses are essential for the well-being and development of any children you have. For example, if your child needs childcare, consider the costs associated with daycare, after-school programs, or babysitters. Include education expenses, such as supplies, school fees, extracurricular activities, or tutoring. Also, remember to include their clothing and medical expenses, especially if your children have special needs.
- *Debt obligations*: When creating your budget, include any debts that must be paid regularly, such as:
  - ✓ Mortgage or rent payments
  - ✓ Car loans
  - ✓ Credit card payments
  - ✓ Student loan payments
  - ✓ Personal loans or any other outstanding debts
- *Insurance*: Include other essential insurance premiums required to protect your family and assets, such as life insurance, homeowner's or renter's insurance, and car insurance.
- *Other essential expenses*: Consider any additional necessary expenses, such as:
  - ✓ Legal and professional fees related to the divorce process
  - ✓ Taxes and tax preparation costs
  - ✓ Personal care products and hygiene items
  - ✓ Pet care expenses, if applicable
- *Non-essential expenses*: You can reduce these discretionary expenses to save money for more essential needs. Non-essential expenses include entertainment, vacations, dining out, travel, recreational activities, gym membership, streaming services, and other non-essential memberships and payments.

Remember, while some non-essential expenses may provide relief or enjoyment, it's *crucial to prioritise essential expenses* when creating a budget after divorce. By carefully considering your financial situation and making conscious spending decisions, you can ensure that your critical needs are met while identifying areas where you can adjust and allocate funds accordingly. Regularly reviewing and revising your budget will help you maintain financial stability and support your post-divorce financial goals.

2. Consider the Impact of Maintenance Payments

The terminology here varies in each jurisdiction, particularly when it comes to maintaining your ex. You may know this as alimony, spousal support, or spouse maintenance. Payments to maintain children are generally known as child support.

If you receive or pay alimony, maintenance, or child support, consider their influence on your budget. If you are the parent receiving these payments, account for them as part of your income. However, be cautious here if your ex is not a consistent payer. If you are responsible for paying alimony, maintenance, or child support, factor them in as fixed expenses.

Understanding your rights to receive maintenance or obligations to pay maintenance to your ex or for the benefit of your children is crucial for accurate budgeting in your financial planning.

3. Review and Adjust Your Spending Habits

As you transition through the divorce, it's vital to reevaluate your spending behaviour and make necessary adjustments. Identify areas where you can reduce flexible spending and find potential savings. This may involve cutting back on unnecessary shopping or entertainment subscriptions. Consider talking to your bank about refinancing debts or restructuring your payments.

This doesn't mean the change is permanent; all you are trying to do is find a plan that works as you gain financial stability. Adopting a mindful and frugal approach to your expenses can free up funds for more pressing financial obligations.

4. Plan for Unexpected Expenses

While creating a budget, remember to factor in unexpected expenses that may arise during and after separation. Unforeseen costs include moving expenses, emergencies, legal fees, or unexpected repairs. Allocate a share of your budget to an emergency fund to handle these unforeseen circumstances without disrupting your overall financial stability.

Aim to save about half a year's worth of living expenses to provide a safety net in case of medical emergencies, job loss, or other unexpected events. Keep this fund separate from your regular savings and only use it for emergencies.

5. Seek Professional Guidance

A financial advisor, accountant, or divorce lawyer can provide valuable insights, help you understand complex financial matters, and offer personalised advice based on your situation. If you feel like you cannot do it on your own, or if there is something you need clarification on, reach out to a professional. Their expertise can be instrumental in developing a budget that suits your needs and goals.

6. Continuously Evaluate and Update Your Budget

Soon, your financial status will change for the better if you stick to your budget and seek more sources of income (which we will discuss later). But, again, life after divorce brings new financial realities, so you must proactively manage your budget. Regularly review and update your budget as circumstances change to reflect any adjustments needed. Continuously assess your income, expenses, and savings to ensure you adequately prepare for whatever life throws at you.

Now that your budget is ready, you may need to find new or more sources of money to cater for all of your expenses. Let's look at how you can do that.

WAYS TO GENERATE INCOME FOR YOUR BUDGET

Here are some things you can do to help you pay your bills:

1. Seek New Employment Opportunities

Even though it's not guaranteed that the new employment opportunities or career advancement plans you seek will come your way soon, they are worth venturing into. So, if you have to invest in acquiring new skills by taking a training program to get that higher-paying job or a promotion, do it. You might not get the money now, but making this decision will come in handy later in life, helping you manage your budget better and work toward financial freedom.

Also, you can look for part-time jobs to help cover some of your expenses, especially the daily bills, allowing you to save more.

2. Alimony or Spousal Support

If you are eligible for alimony or spousal support, consult your lawyer to understand your rights and pursue a fair settlement. Remember that alimony or spousal support is a regular payment provided by one spouse to the other after divorce, aimed at helping the recipient maintain their financial well-being. You should talk to your lawyer about this if you don't have enough income to meet your needs.

3. Child Support

If you have children and are entitled to child support, ensure that you receive the appropriate amount according to the legal guidelines in your jurisdiction. Child support payments help cover raising and caring for your children, lifting some weight off your shoulder and allowing you to invest in other essential things.

4. Sale of Assets

Evaluate your assets and consider selling those that are unnecessary or that you can do without. This may include vehicles, properties, valuable possessions, or investments that can provide a lump sum of cash to supplement your finances. If well managed, this money can kick-start you toward financial stability, as you won't have to depend entirely on your monthly income to pay for everything.

You may find that some of your shared assets need to be sold as part of your divorce settlement. If you and your ex feel that you both will be better off without a particular asset you have together, or neither of you wants to keep it, have your legal teams help you sell it and account for the sale proceeds in your settlement.

5. Financial Assistance Programs

Research and inquire about government assistance programs that may provide financial support in specific situations.

These programs could include:

- Food assistance
- Unemployment benefits
- Healthcare subsidies
- Housing assistance

6. Financial Planning and Investments

Consult with a financial advisor to develop a post-divorce financial plan. They can help you make good decisions concerning savings, investments, and long-term financial goals. Assess your investment portfolio and explore opportunities for growth or diversification to increase your wealth over time.

7. Personal Loans or Credit

Even though you should avoid loans and credits as much as possible, you might be in a position where you need them to survive or invest. So, obtain a personal loan or use credit responsibly to cover immediate or long-term financial needs, if necessary. However, it's crucial to carefully consider the terms, interest rates, and repayment plans to avoid falling into further debt.

Will your income be enough to cover your budget and still pay for your legal and other professional fees during the divorce?

Let's find out.

UNDERSTANDING LEGAL FEES

When going through a divorce, it is essential to understand the legal fees involved and how you can pay for them. Divorce expenses, including court costs, lawyer fees, and other professional fees like financial advisor fees, can accumulate quickly.

If not well planned for, you might use your savings or emergency money to pay for these expenses, impacting your financial future.

This section will provide an understanding of legal divorce fees and explore various payment methods available to individuals navigating the divorce process. It is again important to note that each jurisdiction is different, and you should talk to a divorce lawyer about your own personal circumstances.

So what are the legal fees in divorce?

1. Lawyer Fees

You need to hire a divorce lawyer, so you must start planning for their cost immediately after you realise you are getting a divorce. Usually, they charge their services per hour, and the price varies depending on various factors such as their geographic location, experience, and reputation.

Standard hourly charges vary from some hundred dollars to several hundred dollars, and the total legal fees will be determined by the period the lawyer spends representing you.

2. Retainer Fees

Most divorce lawyers require a downpayment, a retainer fee or payment into a lawyer's trust account. This fee is an advance deposit into the lawyer's trust account that the lawyer will draw from as your case progresses and bills are issued. The lawyer will deduct their hourly fees and other expenses from the retainer, and if it depletes, you will need to top it up for them to continue representing you.

Retainer fees vary significantly depending on different factors. Still, it is usually lower on straightforward divorces and higher on complex divorces involving conflicts about where the children live, significant assets, and other complicated legal issues.

Retainer fees may not cater for all divorce expenses, and you might have to pay additional charges for document preparation, expert consultation, and court costs.

3. Additional Legal Services

Additional legal services may be necessary, depending on the specifics of your divorce. These services may include consultations with specialists such as child experts, real estate appraisers or valuers, or forensic accountants. These experts charge their fees, adding to the total legal expenses.

4. Court Costs and Filing Fees

Other than legal fees, you must also pay filing fees and court costs. These costs vary by jurisdiction and depend on the complexity of your case. Court costs cover several expenses, such as attending hearings, serving papers, and document filing, while filing fees are usually required to initiate divorce proceedings. It's vital to enquire and research the exact charges in your country or state to understand the potential costs involved.

HOW TO PAY FOR LEGAL FEES

Once you have gathered information on the different types of legal fees and the approximate amount you need to cover your divorce process, you can find a way to generate money for legal fees.

Here are ***some of the payment methods you can use***:

- ***Personal savings***: This is a commonly used payment method during divorces. So, if you haven't started saving for these fees, begin immediately, as this method allows you to plan your finances better and minimises the need for external financing or making other inappropriate financial decisions, such as using your investment savings to pay for your divorce.
- ***Payment plans***: Some lawyers may have payment plans, allowing you to spread out the cost of legal fees over time. This plan

permits you to manage your expenses by making systematic payments according to an agreed-upon schedule. During the initial consultation process, inquire if your lawyer offers this payment plan option, as it can help alleviate your financial burden.

- **Personal loans**: If you need quick money for your legal fees, probably because your savings are insufficient or for other reasons, you may consider obtaining a personal loan from a credit union, bank, or other financial organisation. These loans can give you enough money to take care of your divorce-related expenses, and their repayment terms, such as rate and time, can be structured based on your financial situation.
- **Borrowing from friends or family**: You can also borrow your divorce legal fees funds from trusted friends and family members willing and able to support you financially. However, develop clear repayment plans and terms to maintain healthy relationships.
- **Legal aid or pro bono services**: If you have limited financial resources, applying for legal aid or pro bono services may be an option. You can get these services from non-profit organisations, legal clinics, or community centres. These organisations may offer accessible or "affordable" legal assistance based on your income eligibility. However, eligibility and availability principles may vary depending on your country.
- **Divorce funding companies**: Some specific companies have divorce funding deals and services. They provide financial support by settling your legal fees directly to your lawyer. However, they may require a fixed amount or some portion of the settlement in return when the divorce is finalised. It's crucial to evaluate the fees and read the terms associated with such services carefully.

Navigating the financial sides of a divorce is challenging, but with a clear understanding of legal divorce fees and payment options, your experience will be less complicated. Being aware of the potential costs allows you to plan accordingly and explore various payment methods to ensure access to quality legal representation during the divorce process. Remember, making informed decisions considering your short-term and long-term financial plans is essential.

During the divorce process, your goal should be to minimise legal fees and expenses so you have more money for your other plans, and here are some of the ways and approaches that can help save more:

MORE AFFORDABLE DIVORCE APPROACHES

Divorce isn't always about going to court. While you may need a court to approve your agreement or choose to record your agreement in a court order, there are alternatives to litigating your divorce and paying for court hearings and the significant lawyer fees that come with that process.

1. Mediation

This is a collaborative approach where a mediator, usually an unbiased third party, helps simplify negotiations between you and your ex-partner. Mediation is a cost-effective method that eliminates or minimises the need for a traditional litigation approach.

Mediators typically charge an hourly rate or daily rate. The costs will vary depending on where you are and the extent of your dispute. This amount will usually be shared between you and your ex-spouse, making the process more affordable.

2. Collaborative Divorce

In this approach, you both hire divorce lawyers who are collaboratively trained. Instead of commencing court proceedings, you *settle your case outside of court* through cooperation and negotiation. Here, you get to determine if you will split the orange in the middle or whether one party will walk with the juice and the other will take the rind and pulp (to take a well-known collaborative law analogy). When things get tough during negotiations, you might also have to hire child specialists, financial advisors, or other professionals.

By working collaboratively, you can reduce legal costs and reach a settlement that meets the needs of all parties involved. During this divorce approach, it is essential to remember that it is not about what you are entitled to but what you might need most in your life moving forward.

3. Uncontested Divorce

You can agree with your ex-spouse to settle issues such as child arrangements, property division, and child support by yourselves. This approach is sometimes called an uncontested divorce. When you reach an agreement, you avoid extensive court battles and significantly reduce legal expenses.

However, you must include experts, especially divorce lawyers, to help finalise and formalise the divorce process after reaching an agreement.

4. Limited Scope Representation

Also known as unbundled legal services, this approach allows you to **hire a lawyer for specific tasks** rather than full representation. Instead of hiring them for the entire divorce process, you can seek legal assistance for particular aspects of your case, such as legal advice on specific matters or document preparation. You can represent yourself in the parts you don't necessarily need their help with. This approach can help you manage costs by aiming at the areas where you need professional guidance the most.

Research what you need to polish your knowledge and skills for the times you represent yourself. Several online divorce programs and guides will offer information throughout the process. However, even though online advice is cost-effective, ensure you understand your case's implications and legal requirements.

It's crucial to consult with a divorce lawyer to decide the most appropriate method for your situation. A lawyer can guide the feasibility and affordability of each option depending on the specific details of your case.

Chapter 4:

Looking After You

The divorce process might not be done yet, but now that you know how to handle your money worries, you can agree that some weight has been lifted off your shoulders and you can at least sigh with relief.

So, let me suggest something; let's start working on your healing journey. Yes, you are physically and emotionally drained and only you truly know how the divorce has impacted you, so you need to take a break and take care of your well-being.

You might think, *"Is it the right time for me to consider taking a break from everything?"*

Well, here is your answer: **taking care of yourself is not a luxury but a necessity.**

This section will explore the importance of looking after your body, mind, and spirit during divorce. The journey through a divorce requires a remarkable amount of resilience and strength. For you to effectively communicate with your lawyer, make informed decisions about your settlement, and support your children, you must first nurture your well-being. By attending to your physical, mental, and spiritual needs, you will be better equipped to face the obstacles that arise and approach your divorce with a clearer mind and a stronger spirit.

We will learn self-care practices and practical strategies to help you preserve your sanity and balance during this challenging time. We will discuss ways to set boundaries, nurture your mind, and let go of what you cannot control. We will discuss the importance of taking care of your body through proper nutrition, exercise, and avoiding harmful substances. Also, we will delve into the importance of tending to your spirit and finding solace in moments of reflection, faith, and hope.

Remember, self-care is not selfish but an essential investment in your overall well-being. By devoting attention to your mental, spiritual, and physical health, you are nurturing yourself and safeguarding your ability to handle the various aspects of your divorce.

So, let us embark on this section dedicated to exploring the benefits of looking after yourself.

LOOKING AFTER YOUR MIND

To successfully walk through this journey, you must prioritise your mental well-being. This section will explain the importance of that and explore practical strategies to nurture your mind. By implementing the techniques you will learn, you can cultivate a resilient mindset, allowing you to navigate the divorce process with strength and clarity and move on with life. Remember, taking care of your mind is crucial for effectively handling your life's practical and emotional aspects.

So, how exactly will taking a step to care for your mind help you? Let's find out!

What are the benefits of looking after your mind during your divorce process?

1. Improved Emotional Well-being

Lately, anger, sadness, grief, and depression, among other emotions, have probably become the order of your days, but it doesn't have to be that way for the rest of your life. When you take the initiative to care for your mental health, these emotions will gradually reduce and, hopefully, disappear.

Here is an example of how. Suppose you take the time and see a counsellor or therapist. They will help you reflect on yourself and process all these emotions, leading to emotional balance and stability and allowing you to navigate the challenges with resilience. This will, in turn, lead to reduced depression and anxiety, fostering a healthier emotional state overall. By looking after your mental health, you empower yourself to cope with the emotional rollercoaster of divorce and find improved emotional well-being on your journey toward recovery and healing.

2. Improved Decision-making Ability

You enhance cognitive function and emotional regulation by prioritising self-care and implementing strategies to nurture your mind. When your mental well-being is managed, you can approach decision-making with a clearer perspective, free from clouded judgment and overwhelming emotions.

This lets you objectively assess options, consider long-term consequences, and make informed choices aligning with your goals and values. Additionally, taking care of your mental health promotes mental clarity, enabling you to weigh alternatives, see the bigger picture, and navigate the complexities of divorce with certainty and greater confidence.

3. Effective Communication

When you nurture your mind, you better understand everything that is happening. This allows you to express your concerns, needs, and boundaries with empathy and assertiveness. You can engage in constructive and productive conversations with your ex-spouse, lawyers, and other involved parties by managing your emotions and maintaining your mental well-being.

Effective communication facilitates cooperation, understanding, and the potential for amicable resolutions. It also allows you to navigate conflicts with composure, set and maintain healthy boundaries, and ultimately, create a more positive, peaceful, and cooperative environment for yourself and the people around you.

4. Reduced Stress and Anxiety

Mental healthcare practices, such as relaxation techniques, mindfulness, or therapy, help manage anxiety and stress, which are some of the common emotions during divorce. As a result, you can effectively cope with the challenges and uncertainties you face now or later in life.

Taking time for self-reflection and implementing stress-reducing strategies provides:

- A sense of calm
- The ability to approach your situation with emotional stability
- The promotion of a healthier and more balanced state of mind throughout the divorce journey

5. Overall Health and Well-being

Your mental health impacts your physical health. By prioritising your mind, you enhance your overall well-being. For example, when your mind is at ease, and your emotions are under control, you can sleep better, eat better, and experience improved energy levels, which are crucial for effectively handling divorce demands.

6. Future Growth and Adaptability

Looking after your mind during divorce sets the foundation for personal growth and adaptation. It equips you with resilience, empathy, and understanding, enabling you to learn from the experience, embrace change, and move forward positively in your post-divorce life. When your mind is in its best state, you will likely approach life with positivity and hope, opening the doors to more incredible things.

But how do you take care of your mental health?

Here are some strategies that can help support your mental health during this challenging period:

1. Seek Emotional Support

Without a robust support system, you might have difficulty overcoming the overwhelming emotions associated with divorce. So, don't let yourself get lost in your mind; reach out to trusted family members, friends, or a therapist who can provide a safe space, guidance, and a listening ear while you express your emotions and feelings.

An emotional support system can validate your feelings, offer perspectives and coping mechanisms, be your shoulder to lean on, and help you go through this experience with encouragement and understanding. For example, if you are stressed because you don't have someone to pick up your kids from school because you have an appointment with your lawyer, you might be able to turn to a friend. They may offer to help you with the kids, reducing stress and allowing you to go to your meeting with a calmer mind.

2. Practise Self-care

Prioritising self-care is vital during a divorce to maintain your mental well-being.

But what are some of the self-care practices that can help improve your mental health?

- *Having some "me time"*: Carve out moments of solitude in your routine, as they will help you recharge and reflect on your life. Whether taking a walk in nature, meditating, or simply enjoying a cup of tea in silence, give yourself space from everything else and be present in the moment. This will calm your mind and provide you with clarity on different aspects of your life.

- *Engage in physical activity*: Regular physical activities positively affect mental health. So, find activities you enjoy, such as dancing, yoga, exercising, jogging, or swimming. These activities help release stress-reduction hormones called endorphins, improve sleep, and lift your overall mood.
- *Practise relaxation techniques*: Include relaxation practices, such as guided meditation, deep breathing exercises, or progressive muscle relaxation. These techniques can help alleviate stress and anxiety, reduce muscle tension, and promote calmness.
- *Maintain a healthy sleep schedule:* Adequate sleep is vital for mental health. As such, develop a consistent sleep schedule for at least seven hours every night. Also, create a soothing bedtime routine and prioritise good sleep hygiene by creating a comfortable sleep environment, avoiding screens before bed, and practising relaxation techniques to ensure restful sleep.
- *Nourish your body with balanced nutrition*: Pay attention to your diet and ensure you provide your body with nourishing, wholesome foods. Add plenty of vegetables, lean meat, whole grains, and fruits to your meals. Proper nutrition improves mental health and supports overall well-being.
- *Engage in activities you enjoy*: Create some time for the activities that bring you fulfilment and joy. It could be listening to music, pursuing hobbies, reading, engaging in creative outlets, or exploring new interests. These activities bring a sense of relaxation, personal growth, and pleasure, which help boost your mental status.

3. Set Clear Boundaries

Moving forward, you need to create and establish clear boundaries. First, **decide what is acceptable and what is not** regarding interactions and communication with your ex-partner, and ensure to communicate your new boundaries to them. For example, if your ex has developed a habit of visiting anytime they want in the name of "visiting the kids", set boundaries by reminding them that they can only visit on the agreed days or in case of emergencies. Limit contact to minimise emotional distress and triggers if necessary and possible, allowing yourself space to heal.

Secondly, **avoid dealing with or discussing divorce issues at work** to maintain productivity and focus. Create a specific time and space for handling legal divorce-related tasks. For example, have separate email addresses and accounts specifically for communicating with your lawyer and your ex-spouse or their lawyer. This allows you to check and respond to these messages on your terms, preventing them from interrupting your daily routine and work.

By setting these boundaries, you minimise stress, create a sense of control, and ensure that you can dedicate proper attention to your personal and professional life, promoting overall well-being.

4. Let Go of Things Beyond Your Control

As much as you would like to control different aspects of your life, knowing and realising this will sometimes be impossible is essential. For example, your ex's behaviours or actions during the divorce are beyond your reach. The outcomes of divorce court proceedings are beyond your control because if you cannot reach an agreement, the legal systems or judges usually determine the outcome.

Therefore, it is vital to recognise that some aspects of the divorce process and other life matters are beyond your control, and holding on to them only fuels frustration, anxiety, and stress. Instead, **embrace the concept of *surrender*** to free yourself from unnecessary emotional burdens and focus on aspects you can control, such as your emotions, thoughts, and responses. This shift in perspective enables you to cultivate acceptance, release negative energy, and prioritise your well-being, leading to inner peace and greater mental resilience.

5. Focus on Self-reflection

Self-reflection is a self-awareness practice that involves examining and evaluating one's emotions, thoughts, behaviours, beliefs, and experiences. It requires you to turn inward and consciously explore your inner world and personal experiences to understand yourself. This practice often involves asking yourself thought-provoking questions, factoring in past actions and how they impact your life, and considering personal values, goals, and aspirations through journaling or introspection.

Self-reflection will help you understand your emotions better and realise your triggers, empowering positive changes and promoting mental well-being. Also, tuning into your feelings, behaviours, thoughts, experiences, and beliefs will allow you to explore new interests and more desirable coping mechanisms and embrace growth opportunities.

In addition, after examining your feelings, emotions, and thoughts and getting an opportunity to realise new ways to help you improve, you will start accepting the changes brought by divorce, allowing you to move on with your life.

Remember that different ways work best for different people, so find the ones that suit you and incorporate them into your daily life for better results.

Now, let's move on to the next section and learn how to care for your physical body.

LOOKING AFTER YOUR BODY

Since the initial stages of the divorce, you have probably noticed some changes in your body. Maybe you have lost or gained weight, feel more physically exhausted than before, or your skin has become dull, perhaps because you have neglected your skincare routine or due to the many emotional changes you have been experiencing.

But since you have started looking after yourself, it is time to focus on your physical well-being.

This section explores the importance of looking after your body during divorce and discusses various physical activities like walking and yoga to boost mood, manage stress, and cultivate resilience. Maintaining a healthy lifestyle through sleep, stress management, and a balanced diet supports our bodies and emotional well-being. Hydration and nutrition are crucial, while avoiding harmful substances like alcohol and drugs promotes healing. By prioritising physical self-care, you can navigate divorce with greater resilience and a healthier outlook on life.

So, let's dive right in!

Impacts of Prioritising Your Physical Well-being

Looking after your physical well-being during a divorce is crucial for maintaining your overall health and navigating the emotional challenges that arise during this difficult time.

Here are five main points highlighting the significant impacts of prioritising physical self-care:

1. Emotional Resilience

Regular physical activities, like yoga and exercise, can significantly enhance your emotional resilience during a divorce. These activities promote the release of endorphins, natural stress reducers, and mood boosters. Therefore, developing an exercise routine can help improve your emotional well-being and reduce anxiety.

2. Reduces Stress

Since divorce brings immense stress and upheaval into your life, taking care of your physical well-being is essential to reduce stress and promote calmness. Physical activities act as a healthy outlet for stress, allowing you to release frustration and tension. Stress-reducing techniques like deep breathing exercises or meditation can help regulate your stress response and promote emotional stability.

3. Increased Energy and Focus

We've probably said this enough already; divorce is emotionally, physically, and mentally draining, making it critical to maintain high energy levels and mental clarity. Engaging in activities that optimise your body health, such as regular exercise, a balanced diet, and adequate sleep, helps boost your energy levels and enhance your cognitive function. By doing so, you can experience improved concentration, increased productivity, and better decision-making abilities during the divorce process.

4. Improved Self-confidence and Self-image

When your body feels well-rested and looks nice, you will likely love yourself more and have greater self-confidence. In other words, by caring for your body, you nurture yourself more deeply and affirm your value.

This practice can enhance your self-image, providing a solid foundation as you navigate the challenges of divorce. Engaging in activities that make you feel good about yourself can boost your self-esteem and self-worth. You can walk through and past your divorce with your head held high, making you accomplish things you have never imagined before.

5. Improved Overall Well-being

Taking care of your physical well-being during divorce positively impacts your overall well-being. When you prioritise self-care, you invest in your long-term happiness and health. For example, regular exercise and healthy lifestyle choices contribute to improved physical health, better sleep patterns, and a more robust immune system. All these contribute to your overall well-being, enabling you to be better equipped to handle the emotional stressors associated with divorce or other aspects of your life.

In summary, prioritising your physical well-being during a divorce profoundly impacts your emotional and overall well-being. Engaging in physical activities reduces stress, increases energy levels, fosters self-confidence, and improves overall health, contributing to a smoother and more resilient journey through divorce. By nurturing your physical self, you are better equipped to face the emotional challenges and emerge from divorce with resilience.

How Do You Care for Your Physical Well-being?

1. Engage in Regular Exercise

Walking, swimming, jogging, cycling, doing yoga, or enrolling in fitness classes are examples of regular exercise in your daily routine.

Exercises strengthen your bones and muscles, allow you to manage your weight, and improve cardiovascular fitness, contributing to your general well-being.

Exercise is a natural stress reliever that releases endorphins, known as "feel-good" hormones. These hormones can help boost your mood and reduce anxiety. So whenever you feel stressed, take a break from everything and go for a jog or open that online channel and let that guide you through some exercises or yoga practices that will leave you feeling better.

Exercises boost blood circulation, which delivers more nutrients and oxygen, improving stamina, productivity, and skin health.

Divorce disrupts your sleep patterns, making it challenging to get restful sleep. Regular exercise promotes better sleep by helping you fall asleep faster and enjoy more profound, rejuvenating sleep. However, avoid exercising too close to bedtime, which may interfere with sleep.

2. Practise Stress Management Techniques

These techniques include:

- ***Deep breathing exercises***: Practise this technique by inhaling deeply through your nose, filling your belly with air, and exhaling slowly through your mouth for a few minutes every day or whenever you feel overwhelmed. Deep breathing triggers the body's relaxation response, calming the nervous system and reducing stress.
- ***Progressive muscle relaxation***: The muscle relaxation technique involves systematically tensing and releasing different muscle groups to release physical tension and promote relaxation. Start from your toes and work up to your head, tensing each muscle group for a few seconds and then releasing it.
- ***Relaxation techniques***: Explore relaxation techniques such as listening to calming music, taking warm baths, practising aromatherapy, or engaging in hobbies that promote relaxation and provide a mental break from stressors.

All these physical stress management techniques help reduce stress, which translates to improved physical health.

3. Prioritise Sleep

Getting adequate sleep is essential for both physical and emotional well-being.

But how do you ensure you are well-rested every day now that sleepless nights seem like each day's order?

Here is how:

- *Create a regular sleep schedule*: Go to sleep and wake up at a specific time daily.
- *Develop calming bedtime activities*: Engage in comforting activities before bedtime, such as taking a warm shower or bath, reading a book, or practising meditation.
- *Create a sleep-friendly environment*: Make your bedroom quiet, dark, and comfortable.
- *Avoid exposure to screens before bed*: Avoid using electronic gadgets with bright screens (e.g. smartphones, laptops, tablets) for at least an hour before bedtime.
- *Limit stimulants*: Avoid caffeine and nicotine, especially in the evening, as they can affect sleep.
- *Exercise frequently*: Engage in consistent physical activity throughout the day. However, as stated earlier, avoid exercising late in the evening as it can make it difficult to find sleep.
- *Manage stress*: Use relaxation methods like deep breathing or meditation to calm your mind before bed.
- *Avoid excessive fluids and heavy meals before bed:* Consuming excessive fluids and eating a large meal close to bedtime can interfere with sleep.

- *Create a comfortable sleep environment*: Invest in supportive mattresses, pillows, and appropriate bedding to enhance sleep quality.
- *Lessen disruptions*: Have your room free from noise and interruptions that can distract you from sleep.
- *Pursue professional help if needed*: If you have persistent sleep difficulties, consult a healthcare professional or sleep specialist for further evaluation and guidance.

4. Nourish Your Body With Healthy Eating

Proper nutrition is vital for maintaining energy levels, supporting overall well-being, and promoting a healthy mindset.

To ensure you are nourishing your body:

- *Eat a balanced diet*: Embrace a variety of vegetables, fruits, whole grains, healthy fats, and lean proteins in your meals.
- *Portion control*: To avoid overeating and ensure a healthy weight, eat food in small but adequate portion sizes.
- *Stay hydrated*: Take adequate water daily to support general bodily functions.
- *Avoid processed foods*: Reduce or avoid consuming packaged and processed food, which are usually high in added sugars, sodium, and unhealthy fats.
- *Listen to your body*: Pay close attention to your body's fullness and hunger cues, eating when you're hungry and stopping when you're satisfied.
- *Practise mindful eating*: Eat slowly, savour each bite, and be present during meals to enjoy and thoroughly appreciate your food.
- *Avoid drugs and substances and limit alcohol intake*: Consume

alcohol in moderation, as excessive alcohol consumption can negatively affect your health and sleep quality. Also, alcohol and substance use can impair your judgment and cause you to make decisions you might regret later.
- ***Consult a professional***: If you have dietary concerns, seek personalised advice from a registered dietitian.

5. Practise Self-care Activities

Engage in activities that promote self-care and nurture your body.
These include:

- ***Practise good hygiene***: Maintain personal hygiene by regularly bathing, brushing your teeth, and caring for your skin and hair. It may seem silly to mention this, but there may be days when you are so distressed by how things turned out that you cannot get out of bed.
- ***Take breaks and rest***: Listen to your body's signals and take regular breaks from work or other activities to rest and recharge.
- ***Maintain proper posture***: Pay attention to your posture while sitting, standing, and engaging in physical activities to prevent muscle strain and promote overall alignment. Think about the impact bad posture has on your presentation and mood.
- ***Practise self-care rituals:*** Take time for activities that bring you joy and relaxation, such as reading, listening to music, journaling, or engaging in hobbies.
- ***Seek medical care***: Regularly visit healthcare professionals for check-ups and preventive screenings and promptly address health concerns. Also, listen to your body, pay attention to any signs of discomfort, pain, or illness, and seek appropriate medical attention when needed.

All these practices contribute to your physical health and overall well-being, so incorporate them into your daily life for better results. However, it's important to remember everyone's journey through divorce is unique, so it's essential to listen to your body and understand your needs and implement the best techniques.

Now, let's move on to the last section of this chapter, which focuses on looking after your spirit.

LOOKING AFTER YOUR SPIRIT

Numerous strategies can lead to healing as you seek to move forward with life. Apart from looking after your body and mental health in coping with divorce, you must also look after your spirit. Spirit allows you to connect with a higher power than yourself that provides solace, guidance, and a sense of purpose when dealing with difficult circumstances and situations.

This section will explore the impacts of taking care of your spiritual well-being and various ways to look after your spirit during this period and in the future.

Let's get started!

The Impacts of Looking After Your Spirit

When you care for your spiritual health, you will:

1. Attain Emotional Healing and Resilience

Divorce and separation bring forth complex emotions like anger, grief, sadness, and fear. Looking after your spirit allows you to acknowledge and process these emotions, promoting emotional healing and resilience. You will gain clarity and gradually rebuild a sense of inner peace.

2. Find Meaning and Purpose

Divorce has probably disrupted your sense of identity and purpose, leaving you feeling adrift, which is normal.

Caring for your spirit involves exploring and rediscovering your values, passions, and aspirations. Engaging in activities that bring you joy, such as volunteering for a cause you believe in or setting new goals, can help you find meaning and purpose, facilitating personal growth and a renewed sense of direction.

3. Engage in Self-reflection and Self-discovery

By looking after your spirit, you can reconnect with your authentic self, examine your beliefs and values, and evaluate your needs and desires. This introspection allows you to understand yourself better, leading to personal growth and the potential for healthier future relationships.

4. Restore Your Inner Strength and Confidence

Going through a divorce can erode your confidence and self-esteem, leaving you feeling vulnerable. Looking after your spirit involves nurturing self-compassion and practising self-care.

Engaging in spiritual activities that boost your self-confidence, such as going for Bible studies, joining support groups, or listening to your favourite scripture, can help restore your inner strength and belief in your resilience.

5. Cultivate a Positive Outlook

Divorce can create a negative mindset and a sense of hopelessness about the future. By tending to your spirit, you can cultivate a positive outlook. Embracing practices like affirmation, gratitude, or visualisation can shift your perspective and help you focus on the possibilities that lie ahead. Developing positivity nourishes your spirit and empowers you to embrace new beginnings with hope and optimism.

How to Cultivate Your Spiritual Well-being

If you feel lost or uncertain about your future, it probably is because the divorce shook your foundation of beliefs. That is why it is **essential to cultivate your faith and hope**.

How?

To nature your faith and hope, you can seek support from religious or spiritual communities, engage in prayer or meditation, or explore practices that resonate with your beliefs. For example, some people find hope in the serenity prayer: *"God grant me the serenity to understand the things I cannot change, the courage to change things I can, and the wisdom to know the difference."*

By connecting with a higher power or a sense of spirituality, you can find solace and strength to overcome life's challenges. Cultivating faith and hope allows you to envision a better future and restore optimism.

During the turmoil of divorce, **embracing personal beliefs** provides solace and support. It may involve seeking guidance from spiritual leaders, finding comfort in your existing religious community, or exploring new spiritual practices that resonate with your evolving beliefs. Connecting with others with shared experiences, engaging in rituals, or attending support groups can provide a sense of understanding and belonging.

Embracing personal beliefs offers a sanctuary for healing, self-reflection, and navigating the complex emotions that arise during divorce.

The feelings of overwhelmedness, depression, anger, and guilt associated with divorce leave little room for self-reflection. However, **creating quiet spaces for contemplation is crucial** for nurturing your spirit. Find moments of solitude in which you can process and reflect on your emotions.

Whether it's a peaceful corner at home, a local park, or a quiet café, these spaces allow you to reconnect with yourself, find inner strength, and gain clarity. Embrace silence and use it as an opportunity to rediscover your identity, heal, and find a path forward.

Amid the chaos accompanying divorce, ***finding peace and tranquillity*** becomes essential for your spiritual well-being. Engage in activities that bring you joy and serenity. It could be pursuing a hobby, practising mindfulness, immersing yourself in nature, or seeking solace in the arts. These activities create a respite from the stress and uncertainty of divorce, allowing you to rejuvenate your spirit, find comfort, and regain control of your life.

During this challenging time, forgetting all the blessings and good things in your life is easy. That is why you need to **practise gratitude consciously**. Learn to shift your focus from the difficulties and challenges to the blessings and positives in your life.

How?

Take a few moments each day to reflect on what you are grateful for. Write these things down in a gratitude journal, express them verbally to yourself or others, or hold them in your thoughts. Focus on the small blessings, joys, and acts of kindness that bring positivity to your life.

Doing this helps you recognise the abundance and beauty that still exist, fostering a sense of appreciation and contentment. Gratitude opens your heart to compassion, forgiveness, and acceptance, allowing you to relinquish resentment and embrace a more spiritual perspective. It connects you to something greater than yourself, whether it's a higher power, the universe, or the interconnectedness of all beings, providing solace, hope, and strength during the divorce journey.

Chapter 5:

It's No Time for Game Playing

In the journey of divorce, it is essential to recognise that this is not the time for games. Every decision, every action, and every behaviour carries weight and has the potential to shape the outcome of your divorce and impact your future. This chapter serves as a guiding light, highlighting the significance of taking this process seriously and navigating it gracefully. It provides invaluable principles that will help you make informed choices, avoid common pitfalls, and ensure a smoother transition into the next chapter of your life.

Let's dive into the principles that should guide you through this challenging journey.

REVENGE IS NOT THE ANSWER

"Revenge is a dish best served cold," they say. But when it comes to divorce, revenge is not the answer. As tempting as it may be to seek vengeance, to make your ex-partner feel the pain they have caused you, it's important to remember that revenge only perpetuates a cycle of negativity and prolongs the healing process. However, you may wonder, *"Why shouldn't I get revenge after all they have done to me?"*

Well, here is why:

1. Revenge Causes an Emotional Drain

Focusing on revenge during a divorce is emotionally draining. It keeps you in a negative mindset, constantly reliving the pain and anger. Directing your energy towards revenge depletes your emotional resources and hinders your healing process. Instead, shifting your focus towards self-care and personal growth allows you to rebuild and move forward.

2. Prolonged Conflict

Seeking revenge leads to a never-ending cycle of conflict. It fuels hostility and escalates tensions between you and your ex-partner, creating a toxic environment that affects you and any children involved. Breaking free from this cycle promotes a healthier environment and creates more productive and amicable interactions.

3. Legal Complications

Engaging in vengeful actions can have severe legal consequences. It may jeopardise arrangements for children, property settlements, and even your reputation. Courts value cooperation and the ability to co-parent effectively, so it's crucial to approach divorce proceedings with a focus on resolution rather than retaliation.

4. Stagnation of Personal Growth

Revenge keeps you stuck in the past, preventing personal growth and hindering your ability to create a better future. By holding onto anger and resentment, you deny yourself the opportunity to heal, learn from the experience, and embrace new beginnings. Redirecting your energy towards self-improvement and personal goals empowers you to evolve and thrive beyond divorce.

5. Impact on Well-being

Focusing on revenge takes a toll on your mental and physical well-being. It increases stress levels, disrupts sleep patterns, and hampers overall health. Choosing a path of forgiveness and letting go allows you to prioritise your well-being and create a positive, fulfilling life post-divorce.

Remember, revenge may provide temporary satisfaction but ultimately prolongs the pain and hinders your growth. Embracing forgiveness, healing, and focusing on your well-being will lead you to a brighter and more fulfilling future. Buddha once said, *"Holding onto anger is like drinking poison and expecting the other person to die."*

How to Forgive and Avoid Vengeance

Trust me. I know how hard it can be to forgive someone who has caused you pain and stress. However, it is doable and worth it.

Here are a few tips to help you ignore the temptation and avoid falling into the trap of vengeance:

- ***Acknowledge your emotions***: Recognise and accept the range of emotions you may be experiencing, including anger, betrayal, and sadness. Understand that these emotions are natural and valid responses to the situation. Acknowledging and validating your feelings can start the healing process and help you to move toward forgiveness.
- ***Shift your perspective***: Try to view the divorce from a different perspective. Instead of seeing it as a personal attack or a battle to win, consider it a transition to a new chapter in your life. Reframe the situation as an opportunity for personal growth and a chance to create a more fulfilling future.
- ***Practise self-compassion***: Be gentle and compassionate towards yourself during this challenging time. Understand that forgiveness is a process, and it takes time. Observe patience, understanding, and self-care as you navigate the emotions associated with divorce. Forgiveness is not about condoning your ex-spouse's actions but rather about releasing the emotional burden that revenge brings.
- ***Seek support***: Surround yourself with a robust support system that includes friends, family, or a therapist who can provide

guidance and empathy. Sharing your feelings and experiences with trusted individuals can help you gain perspective and find healthy outlets for your emotions. They can also offer a different viewpoint that encourages forgiveness and moving forward.

- *Focus on personal growth*: Direct your energy towards personal growth and self-improvement instead of seeking revenge. Explore new interests, set goals, and invest in your well-being. By shifting your attention to self-development, you divert your focus from the negative aspects of the divorce and create a positive path toward your future.
- *Practise empathy*: Try to understand the perspective of your ex-spouse. While it may be challenging, putting yourself in their shoes can help you develop empathy and compassion. Recognise that everyone makes mistakes and has their struggles. Cultivating empathy can facilitate the process of forgiveness and promote a more peaceful resolution.
- *Letting go of resentment*: Clinging to resentment only prolongs your suffering. Choose to release the anger and bitterness that may be holding you back. Forgiveness is a gift you offer yourself, releasing you from the burden of vengeance and allowing you to move forward.

DON'T BE AN OSTRICH

During a divorce, it's crucial not to adopt an ostrich-like approach and bury your head in the sand, avoiding the issues. This is not the time for games or avoidance. Although it may seem overwhelming, confronting the challenges head-on is the only way to move forward and create a better future. By ignoring or delaying the necessary actions and decisions, you may inadvertently make the situation worse. Instead, muster the courage to face the issues, have difficult conversations, and make the necessary choices to ensure a smoother transition. Remember that by addressing these challenges now, you are paving the way for a fresh start and a more fulfilling life beyond divorce.

Tips on How to Address Issues Instead of Avoiding Them

Here are some tips on how you can avoid being like an ostrich and instead face issues head-on:

- *Face your emotions*: Acknowledge and process your emotions rather than ignoring or suppressing them. Allow yourself to grieve, feel anger, or experience sadness. Seek support from a therapist or counsellor who can guide you through this emotional journey. For example, instead of avoiding your anger towards your ex-spouse, take the time to understand and express your emotions healthily. This might involve journaling, talking to a trusted friend, or attending support groups.
- *Seek professional guidance*: Consult with professionals specialising in divorce-related matters, such as lawyers, mediators, or therapists. They can provide valuable advice and guidance tailored to your situation. For example, if you're hesitant to address financial issues, seek the expertise of a financial planner or accountant who can help you navigate the complexities of dividing assets, understanding financial implications, and planning for your future.
- *Communicate effectively*: Open and honest communication is vital to resolving conflicts and finding solutions. Express your needs, concerns, and boundaries clearly, while also being receptive to the perspectives of others. For example, initiate respectful and constructive dialogue instead of avoiding

difficult conversations about parenting arrangements with your ex-spouse. Focus on finding a compromise that prioritises the well-being of your children.

- *Prioritise self-care*: Take good care of yourself emotionally, physically, and mentally. Embrace activities that promote relaxation, self-reflection, and personal growth. This will help you maintain a strong foundation as you navigate the challenges of divorce. For example, create a self-care routine with exercise, meditation, leisure, or hobbies that bring you joy. These practices can provide a sense of balance and rejuvenation during challenging times.
- *Take proactive steps*: Break down overwhelming tasks into manageable steps and take action. Addressing one issue at a time can prevent you from feeling overwhelmed and encourage a sense of progress. For example, create a checklist of tasks and deadlines instead of avoiding the paperwork and legal processes involved in your divorce. Dedicate specific time slots to tackle each item on the list, ensuring you make consistent progress.

Remember, by actively addressing the issues rather than avoiding them, you empower yourself to make informed decisions and move forward with clarity and confidence. Facing the challenges head-on allows you to navigate the divorce process more effectively and ultimately create a better future.

MAKE UP YOUR MIND

During your divorce, you must develop the ability to make up your mind and stick to your decisions. Continually changing your mind can complicate the process and create challenges for your legal and financial advisors, who rely on your instructions. It can also cost you money. By adopting a decisive mindset, you can guide your advisors clearly, ensuring everyone is working towards the same goals. Making up your mind and maintaining a consistent stance helps streamline divorce proceedings and minimises confusion and conflicts. It demonstrates your confidence and assertiveness, allowing you to take control of your journey and move forward purposefully.

How to Be Decisive

Here are some tips to help you make up your mind and stick to your decisions:

- *Gather information and consider options*: You can weigh the available options and make informed decisions by thoroughly researching and understanding your situation. Having all the necessary information reduces uncertainty and allows you to assess the potential outcomes, making it easier to choose the path that aligns with your goals. For example, if you are considering different arrangements for your children, research the pros and cons of each option, consult with a family therapist, and understand the needs and well-being of your children before making a decision.
- *Clarify your priorities and values*: Identifying your priorities and values provides a framework for decision-making. When you clearly understand what matters most to you, it becomes easier to assess different choices based on how well they align with your core beliefs. This clarity empowers you to make decisions true to yourself and your desired future. For instance, if maintaining a peaceful co-parenting relationship with your

ex-spouse is a priority, you should prioritise compromise and open communication over contentious legal battles.

- ***Trust your intuition***: Your intuition can be a powerful guiding force in decision-making. By tapping into your instincts and listening to your inner voice, you can access valuable insights that may not be apparent through logical analysis alone. Trusting your intuition helps you navigate the complexities of divorce with a sense of authenticity and self-assurance. For example, if a proposed financial settlement seems advantageous but doesn't seem quite right, trust your intuition and seek further clarification or renegotiation.
- ***Set realistic expectations***: Recognising that divorce involves compromises and trade-offs allows you to approach decision-making with a realistic mindset. By understanding that perfection is not attainable, you can let go of the pressure to make the "perfect" choice and instead focus on finding resolutions that meet your needs and contribute to a positive future. For instance, when dividing assets, be prepared to prioritise certain items or properties and accept that you may need to let go of others.
- ***Seek emotional support***: Having a supportive network provides emotional validation and guidance during the decision-making process. By sharing your thoughts and concerns with trusted individuals, you can gain different perspectives and insights to bolster your decision-making confidence. Emotional support helps you feel more grounded and empowered, enabling you to move forward with clarity.

By implementing these tips, you can enhance your ability to be decisive throughout your divorce.

BEING RIGHT ISN'T THE ANSWER

During a divorce, pursuing being right at all costs often leads to unnecessary conflict and hinders the overall process. Instead of fixating on winning every argument, it is essential to shift the focus towards achieving a smooth divorce, prioritising the welfare of children, and ensuring a fair financial outcome. While it can be tempting to engage in battles to prove a point, this approach prolongs the emotional distress and can negatively impact the well-being of everyone involved. By redirecting your energy towards finding common ground, seeking compromise, and maintaining open communication, you create an environment conducive to resolving issues amicably.

ACCEPT YOUR PART IN THE STORY

You must recognise and accept your part in the story during a divorce. While it may be natural to feel wronged or treated unfairly, it is important to acknowledge that no one is perfect, including yourself. By owning your actions and behaviours, you can cultivate a sense of self-reflection and personal growth. This acknowledgment allows for a shift in perspective, fostering empathy and understanding toward your ex-spouse's point of view. Instead of clinging to bitterness and resentment, approaching the divorce with a sense of self-awareness opens the door to constructive communication and the possibility of finding common ground. By accepting your part in the story, you pave the way for a more amicable and transformative divorce process, leading to a healthier and more empowered post-divorce life.

Now, *how do you accept your part in the story?* How do you acknowledge that you were wrong too?

- ***Self-reflection***: Reflect on your actions, behaviours, and choices throughout the marriage. Consider positive and negative aspects and how they may have contributed to the relationship dynamics. For example, you might recognise that your lack of communication or failure to address specific issues contributed to the marriage breakdown.
- ***Seek feedback***: Be open to feedback from trusted friends, family, or therapists. Ask for their honest perspectives on your role in the marriage and the events leading to the divorce. This external insight can help you gain a more objective understanding of your actions and their impact. For instance, a friend might share how they observed situations where you could have been more patient or understanding.
- ***Take responsibility***: Accept responsibility for your mistakes and shortcomings. Acknowledge any hurtful actions or behaviours you displayed during the marriage. For example, you might realise that your defensiveness or lack of emotional support affected the relationship. Taking responsibility allows you to move from a position of blame to one of personal growth and accountability.
- ***Apologise and make amends***: If appropriate, sincerely apologise to your ex-spouse for any pain or harm you may have caused. Apologies can create an understanding environment and facilitate a more cooperative divorce process. For instance, you may apologise for not being fully present in the relationship or not fulfilling certain expectations.
- ***Learn and grow***: Use divorce as an opportunity for personal growth and development. Identify areas where you can improve as an individual and partner in future relationships. For example, you might realise the need to work on your communication skills or develop better conflict-resolution strategies.

By following these tips, you can actively own your part in the story and approach the divorce with a mindset of personal growth and understanding. Remember, owning your part does not mean taking the blame for everything but instead recognising your contributions to the dynamics of the marriage.

YOU DO NOT KNOW EVERYTHING

During a divorce, you must recognise that you don't know everything. Adopting a know-it-all attitude can hinder effective communication and problem-solving, making it challenging for others, including legal advisors, to reason with you. Being a know-it-all can be seen as stubbornness or resistance to alternative perspectives, potentially impeding the progress of negotiations or settlements. It's crucial to approach the divorce process with an open mind and be willing to listen to the advice and expertise of professionals with experience navigating divorce-related matters.

It's worth acknowledging that the need to be a know-it-all can stem from a trauma response to the divorce. The pain and vulnerability experienced during this time may drive you to adopt a strong and in-control persona as a protective mechanism. By portraying yourself as all-knowing, you may camouflage your deeper emotions and create a sense of security. However, it's essential to recognise that true strength lies in acknowledging and addressing your emotions rather than suppressing them. Embracing vulnerability allows you to seek the necessary support and guidance to navigate the divorce process more effectively, leading to a healthier and more favourable outcome.

Tips on How to Avoid Being a Know-it-all

Sometimes, you may be displaying the know-it-all persona without even realising it. To avoid doing so, follow these tips:

- *Practise open-mindedness*: Keep an open mind and be willing to consider different perspectives and ideas. Understand that you may not have all the answers or possess all the knowledge about legal and financial matters. Listen attentively to the advice and suggestions of your legal advisors and be receptive to their expertise. For example, if your lawyer suggests a particular approach for negotiating a settlement, take the time to understand their reasoning and consider the potential benefits before dismissing their advice based solely on your assumptions.
- *Seek professional guidance*: Rely on the expertise of professionals who specialise in divorce-related matters. Engage with your legal team, financial advisors, and therapists, who can provide valuable insights and guidance. Trust their knowledge and experience, recognising that they have dealt with numerous divorce cases and understand the intricacies involved. For instance, if a financial expert advises you on the best way to divide shared assets, be willing to listen and consider their recommendations, even if they differ from your initial assumptions.
- *Foster effective communication*: Focus on maintaining open and respectful communication with your ex-spouse and legal team. Avoid adopting an argumentative or defensive attitude when discussing crucial matters. Practise active listening and strive to understand the perspectives of others involved. For instance, during discussions about arrangements for your children, listen attentively to the concerns and needs of your ex-spouse, acknowledging that their input is crucial for reaching a fair and mutually agreeable solution.
- *Reflect on emotions and triggers*: Take the time to reflect on your emotional state and triggers that may contribute to a know-it-all mentality. Recognise that the need to appear knowledgeable

and in control may be driven by underlying fears, anxieties, or a desire to protect yourself. By acknowledging and addressing these emotions, you can work towards a more balanced and constructive approach to divorce. For example, if you become defensive or argumentative during negotiations, take a step back, reflect on the underlying emotions being triggered, and consider seeking support from a therapist or counsellor to help you navigate these challenges.

By implementing these tips, you can avoid the know-it-all trap and create a more collaborative and effective environment during your divorce.

WHAT IF YOUR EX DOESN'T COOPERATE?

During a divorce, your ex-spouse may prove difficult and uncooperative despite your best efforts to make the process smooth and amicable. In such situations, staying resilient and focusing on finding solutions is essential.

Here are some options to help you navigate through that challenging dynamic.

Maintain patience and a calm demeanour, even in the face of complex behaviour from your ex-spouse. By **remaining composed**, you can avoid escalating conflicts and create an environment more conducive to productive discussions. For instance, if your ex-spouse is unresponsive to your requests for information, resist the temptation to react impulsively and instead give them time to gather the necessary documents or respond to your inquiries.

- Learn to ***recognise signs of uncooperative behaviour*** and understand any underlying motivations. This can help you anticipate potential obstacles and adjust your approach accordingly. For example, suppose your ex-spouse consistently avoids discussions or becomes defensive when specific topics arise. In that case, it may indicate a need for professional mediation or a shift in your communication strategy.

- While patience is valuable, *there may come a point where you need to take bold action to move the process forward*. Seek assistance from your legal team or engage a mediator to facilitate negotiations. For instance, if attempts at amicable discussions repeatedly fail and your ex-spouse refuses to cooperate in critical decision-making, consulting with your lawyer and exploring alternative dispute resolution methods can help break the impasse.
- *Be proactive in providing all necessary documents and information* to address any questions or concerns from your ex-spouse or their legal representatives. Being transparent and forthcoming can help build trust and minimise unnecessary conflicts. For example, promptly sharing financial statements, property documentation, or other relevant records can demonstrate your willingness to cooperate and promote a calmer process. Sharing family photographs can go a long way to smooth the way.
- Recognise that not every issue will be resolved in your favour, and choosing your battles is essential. *Allowing some concessions or compromises on more minor matters* can help maintain a sense of growth and goodwill. For instance, if disagreements arise over minor aspects of the settlement, consider finding common ground and be willing to make small concessions that ultimately contribute to a more favourable resolution.

Let's move on to the next chapter and learn about the power of your attitude during divorce.

Chapter 6:

Attitude Is Everything

Amid the stormy seas of divorce, where emotions run high and uncertainty looms large, one beacon of light remains within your control – your attitude. As you navigate the challenging path toward a new chapter in your life, it's crucial to recognise the power your attitude holds. Attitude is the compass that guides you through the darkest nights, the force that propels you forward when the road seems unbearable.

In this chapter, we will delve into the significance of attitude and explore practical strategies to check and manage your perspective and cultivate a positive outlook that will aid you in gracefully surviving the trials of your divorce. Remember, even in adversity, you can transform your mindset and embrace the power of decisive grace.

Let us embark on this transformative journey together, uncovering the secrets to adopting an unwavering and resilient attitude throughout the challenges.

SIGNS THAT YOU NEED TO SHIFT YOUR ATTITUDE

Recognising the signs of a negative attitude during your divorce is crucial to shift toward a more positive mindset.

Here are some signs that indicate you may have a negative attitude and that it's time to make a change:

Suppose you find yourself **consistently dwelling on the negative aspects** of your divorce, replaying negative conversations or events in your mind. In that case, it's a sign that your attitude may lean toward the negative. This pattern of rumination can keep you stuck in a cycle of negativity and hinder your ability to move forward.

If you constantly feel **consumed by bitterness, resentment, or a desire for revenge**, it's a clear sign that negativity has taken hold of your attitude. These emotions can be toxic and prevent you from healing and finding peace.

Suppose you constantly *feel stuck in a sense of helplessness or victimhood*. In that case, it indicates a negative attitude that hinders your ability to take control of your life and make positive changes.

It may indicate a negative attitude if you withdraw from friends, family, or support networks and *isolate yourself during your divorce*. Isolation can intensify negative emotions and limit opportunities for healing and growth.

If you *struggle to find joy or experience positive emotions*, negativity has overshadowed your mindset, leading to low motivation, low energy levels, and dissatisfaction.

Recognising these signs and actively working towards shifting your negative attitude is a vital step towards maintaining a positive mindset during your divorce. By challenging negative thoughts, seeking support, and focusing on personal growth, you can gradually cultivate a more positive attitude that will help you navigate the process with grace and resilience.

MAINTAINING A POSITIVE ATTITUDE

Divorce can be incredibly challenging and emotionally draining, but maintaining a positive attitude throughout can make a difference. It's important to remember that staying positive doesn't mean you must always plaster on a smile or pretend everything is perfect. It's about approaching the situation with a mindset that looks for the silver lining and possibilities for growth, even when things seem tough. As the saying goes, *"Life is 10% what happens to us and 90% how we react to it."*

Sure, staying positive during a divorce can sometimes feel like doing a marathon while juggling flaming torches, but trust me, it's worth the struggle. By embracing a positive attitude, you find strength within yourself that you never knew existed. It's like having a little cheerleader in your corner, whispering encouraging words in your ear even when you feel like giving up. Maya Angelou once said, *"If you don't like something, change it. If you can't change it, change your attitude."* Remember, you have the power to choose how you respond to the challenges that come your way, and maintaining a positive mindset can be a powerful tool in helping you navigate the rocky terrain of divorce.

By adhering to the following tips, you can maintain a positive attitude and get through your divorce with grace:

1. Start by Checking Your Attitude

Regularly checking your attitude lets you stay attuned to your emotional well-being and make necessary adjustments. It empowers you to take control of your mindset and consciously choose a positive outlook, even in the face of adversity.

Awareness of your attitude is the first step towards making conscious changes and maintaining a positive attitude throughout your divorce journey.

To check your attitude:

- Take moments throughout the day or set aside specific times to pause and reflect on the general tone of your thoughts.
- Consider whether you tend to focus on challenges, setbacks, or negative aspects of your divorce or if you prioritise opportunities for growth and a new beginning.
- Gain clarity on patterns and tendencies in your attitude and recognise negative thought patterns or emotional triggers that hinder a positive mindset.

2. Understand and Accept Your Part in the Separation

Understanding and accepting your part in the separation is crucial to maintaining a positive attitude during a divorce. It involves acknowledging your role in the relationship breakdown and taking responsibility for your actions and choices. Doing so empowers you to rise above negative behaviour and work towards personal growth and a better future.

Acknowledging your part in the divorce requires honesty and self-reflection. It may involve examining the relationship dynamics, your behaviours, and your choices that contributed to the separation. This process can be challenging and may bring up difficult emotions, but it is an essential step toward healing and growth.

Taking responsibility for your actions means owning up to the mistakes or shortcomings that may have impacted the marriage. It does not imply self-blame or wallowing in guilt but instead recognising the areas where you could have done better and learning from them. By accepting your part, you release the need to play the victim and instead empower yourself to make positive changes.

3. Rise Above Negative Behaviours

Rising above negative behaviour is an essential aspect of maintaining a positive outlook. It means refraining from engaging in destructive behaviours, such as seeking revenge or perpetuating conflicts. Instead, focus on personal growth and self-improvement. Use this time of transition to develop new skills, explore your passions, and invest in your well-being. You create a path towards a positive future by shifting your focus from dwelling on past mistakes to actively working on self-improvement.

4. Choose Forgiveness

Moving forward with grace is about cultivating a mindset of forgiveness, compassion, and resilience. It involves doing away with resentments and bitterness, which only weigh you down. By embracing grace, you approach the divorce process and interactions with your former partner with dignity and respect. This attitude shift benefits your emotional well-being and sets a positive tone for navigating divorce's legal, logistical, and emotional aspects.

5. Write a Journal

Writing a journal during a divorce is a powerful tool for maintaining a positive attitude and navigating the emotional challenges that arise. Journaling provides a safe and private space to express your thoughts, feelings, and experiences, allowing you to process emotions and prevent rumination.

When you write in a journal:

- You allow yourself to explore and release any pent-up negativity or overwhelming emotions.
- It provides an outlet for your thoughts and feelings, offering a non-judgmental space in which to pour out your heart.
- You create distance between yourself and the intensity of your emotions, enabling you to gain clarity and perspective.

Journaling helps you make sense of your experiences and **_can lead to valuable insights and personal growth_**. As you write, you may uncover patterns, recurring themes, or underlying emotions you were unaware of. This self-reflection allows you to better understand your emotions, triggers, and reactions. It can help you identify areas for personal development and places where you can let go or find forgiveness.

Moreover, journaling ***provides a tangible record of your progress*** and growth throughout the divorce. As time passes, you can reflect on earlier entries and see how far you have come. This reflection can be empowering and provide a sense of accomplishment. It reminds you of the strength and resilience you have demonstrated, helping you maintain a positive attitude even in challenging times.

By regularly writing in a journal, you create a structured practice of self-care and self-reflection. It becomes a ritual that allows you to check in with yourself, process emotions, gain clarity, and release negativity. It's important to note that there are no rules for journaling. You can write freely, focusing on whatever comes to mind, or use prompts or specific techniques if they resonate with you.

6. Exercise

Engaging in regular exercise during a divorce can have a profound impact on both your physical and mental well-being. Exercise is known to release endorphins, which are natural chemicals in the brain that enhance mood and reduce stress. By incorporating exercise into your routine, you can promote a positive mindset and better cope with the challenges of divorce.

Physical activity acts as a natural stress reliever. When you exercise, your body releases endorphins, creating happiness and well-being. This chemical response can help counteract the negative emotions and stress associated with divorce. Exercise also stimulates the production of serotonin, a neurotransmitter that plays a key role in regulating mood, sleep, and appetite. Increasing serotonin levels through exercise can improve your overall emotional state and contribute to a more positive outlook.

Regular exercise can also serve as a healthy distraction from the emotional turmoil of divorce. It provides a focused and productive outlet for pent-up energy and emotions. Engaging in physical activity allows you to temporarily shift your attention away from the challenges and uncertainties of divorce and channel your energy towards something positive and beneficial for your body.

Finding an activity that you enjoy is crucial for maintaining consistency and motivation. It could be anything that gets your body moving and brings you joy. Whether it is walking, jogging, swimming, dancing, yoga, or participating in a team sport, choose an activity that resonates with you and fits your preferences and physical abilities. The key is to engage in exercise that you look forward to, bringing you a sense of fulfilment and satisfaction.

In addition to its immediate mood-boosting effects, exercise also offers long-term benefits for your mental health. Regular physical activity is effective in reducing the symptoms of anxiety and depression, improving sleep quality, enhancing self-esteem, and increasing resilience to stress. By investing time and effort into exercise, you are investing in your overall well-being and equipping yourself with valuable tools to navigate the emotional challenges of divorce.

Remember that exercise doesn't have to be overly strenuous or time-consuming. Even short bursts of activity can have significant benefits. Start with small, achievable goals and gradually increase your activity level as you build stamina and confidence. Incorporating exercise into your daily routine will contribute to a positive mindset during your divorce and promote your overall physical and mental health, allowing you to emerge more robust and resilient from this life transition.

7. Seek Support

Seeking support during a divorce is essential for maintaining a positive attitude and navigating the emotional rollercoaster accompanying this challenging life transition. Building a support network can provide guidance, encouragement, and a sense of belonging during this difficult time.

One of the most valuable forms of support comes from friends and family. Contact trusted individuals offering a listening ear, empathy, and understanding. Sharing your thoughts, feelings, and concerns with loved ones allows you to release emotional burdens and gain perspective. They can provide a fresh outlook, offer insights, and remind you of your strengths and resilience. Their support can provide comfort, reassurance, and motivation to keep moving forward with a positive mindset.

As well as talking to friends and family, consider ***seeking professional support from a therapist or counsellor.*** A trained professional can provide a safe and non-judgmental space for you to express your emotions, process your experiences, and gain valuable insights. Therapists can offer guidance, coping strategies, and tools to help you navigate the complexities of divorce. They can also help you develop healthy coping mechanisms, manage stress, and cultivate a positive attitude. Therapy can be a transformative experience, providing the tools and support needed to heal and grow during this challenging time.

Being part of a ***support group or community*** can be immensely beneficial. Connecting with others who are going through or have been through divorce allows you to share experiences, exchange advice, and gain a sense of camaraderie. These groups offer a supportive and understanding environment where you can find solace, encouragement, and practical tips for coping with the challenges of divorce. Engaging with others who have walked a similar path can be empowering and help you maintain perspective and a positive attitude.

Remember, seeking support is not a sign of weakness but rather an acknowledgment of your strength and a proactive step toward healing and growth. Surrounding yourself with a supportive network is vital during this transitional period. It offers emotional support, practical guidance, and a sense of belonging. Having someone to talk to, lean on, and share your journey with can help you maintain perspective, find strength in difficult times, and cultivate a positive attitude as you navigate the complexities of divorce.

8. Practise Self-care

Prioritise self-care activities that nurture your mind, body, and spirit, including meditation, relaxing baths, indulging in hobbies, or engaging in activities that bring you joy and relaxation.

Taking care of yourself reinforces a positive mindset and strengthens your resilience in the following ways.

Self-care activities *provide a space in which you can process and manage emotions*. You can release pent-up emotions, gain clarity, and cultivate emotional resilience by meditating, journaling, or talking to a trusted friend or therapist. This emotional well-being contributes to a positive attitude by allowing you to approach challenges with a calmer and more balanced perspective.

Divorce can be a highly stressful and overwhelming experience. Engaging in self-care activities such as exercise, deep breathing exercises, or relaxing baths *helps reduce stress levels*. When stress is reduced, you can better maintain a positive attitude and cope with the difficulties of divorce more effectively.

Prioritising self-care ensures you care for your physical and mental energy levels. You *recharge and replenish your energy reserves* by engaging in activities that bring joy, relaxation, and fulfilment. This renewed energy allows you to approach challenges with a clearer mind, increased focus, and a positive outlook.

Self-care practices *foster a sense of self-worth and self-compassion*. You reinforce positive beliefs about yourself by prioritising your well-being and engaging in activities that make you feel good. This heightened self-esteem contributes to a positive attitude as you navigate the divorce process, helping you maintain confidence and resilience.

Self-care provides a break from the stresses and challenges of divorce. Engaging in activities you enjoy allows you to shift your focus away from the difficulties momentarily and ***allows you to recharge***. Taking time for yourself helps prevent burnout and enables you to approach the divorce process with renewed motivation and positivity.

Self-care practices ***can help shift your mindset towards positivity***. Engaging in activities that bring you joy, relaxation, and a sense of fulfilment boosts your mood and reinforces positive emotions. It helps redirect your attention to the present moment, allowing you to appreciate the positive aspects of your life despite the difficulties of divorce.

9. Focus on Personal Growth

Focusing on personal growth during a divorce can be a transformative and empowering experience. This transitional period offers an opportunity to reflect on your life, reassess your priorities, and set goals for your future.

You can focus on your personal growth in the following ways.

Define clear and meaningful goals for yourself. These short-term and long-term goals cover various aspects of your life, such as career, relationships, health, or personal interests. Setting goals provides a sense of direction and purpose, giving you something positive to focus on amidst the difficulties of divorce.

Use this transitional period to ***expand your knowledge and acquire new skills***. Enrol in courses or workshops that align with your interests or career aspirations. Learning something new stimulates your mind, boosts your self-confidence, and opens doors to new opportunities. It serves as a reminder of your capacity for growth and personal achievement.

Engage in activities that bring you joy and fulfilment. ***Dedicate time to hobbies, creative pursuits, or recreational activities*** that allow you to express yourself and tap into your passions. Immersing yourself in activities you love promotes a positive mindset, enhances well-being, and reinforces a sense of purpose and joy.

Prioritise your physical and mental well-being during this transformative period. ***Explore practices that enhance your overall health,*** such as adopting a regular exercise routine, practising mindfulness or meditation, maintaining a balanced diet, and getting enough restful sleep. Taking care of your well-being contributes to a positive attitude, strengthens your resilience, and equips you to face the challenges of divorce with greater clarity and strength.

Be ***open to new opportunities and experiences*** that come your way. Step out of your comfort zone and embrace change. Trying new things expands your perspective, builds resilience, and fosters personal growth. Whether travelling, meeting new people, or engaging in unfamiliar activities, these experiences can be transformative and reinforce a positive outlook.

Focusing on personal growth during a divorce allows you to channel your energy into something positive and meaningful. It helps shift your focus away from the difficulties and challenges, fostering optimism and a sense of purpose. Embracing personal development empowers you to emerge stronger, wiser, and more resilient from divorce, ready to embrace the next chapter of your life with grace and optimism.

10. Gratitude Practice

Cultivating a gratitude practice during your divorce can be a powerful tool for maintaining a positive mindset and finding moments of joy and appreciation amidst the challenges.

Here are some practical steps to help you cultivate gratitude during this difficult time:

Acknowledge even the smallest things you are thankful for. It might be as simple as a stunning sunset, a moment of peace, or a kind gesture from a friend. Train your mind to look for the positive aspects, no matter how small or seemingly insignificant they may be.

Commit a few minutes every day to ***noting down things you are thankful for in a journal.*** Reflect on the positive experiences, acts of kindness, personal growth, or moments of joy you've experienced. Writing them down helps solidify the gratitude in your mind and allows you to revisit them whenever you need a reminder of the positive things in your life.

Incorporate ***mindfulness*** into your gratitude practice by being fully present in the moment. When you encounter something that brings you joy or gratitude, pause and immerse yourself in that experience. Notice the details, sensations, and associated emotions to deepen your connection to the positive aspects and reinforce your gratitude.

Focusing on the challenges and difficulties is natural during a divorce. However, consciously try to ***shift your mindset*** towards the positive aspects. Instead of dwelling on what you have lost, redirect your attention to what you still have and the opportunities for personal growth and new beginnings.

View your divorce as an ***opportunity for growth and self-discovery.*** Recognise the lessons you've learned and the strength you've gained throughout the process. Express gratitude for the personal growth, resilience, and newfound wisdom you have acquired from this challenging experience.

Take the time to ***express your appreciation for those who have supported you during this difficult time.*** Reach out to friends, family members, or professionals who have provided guidance and support, and let them know how grateful you are for their presence in your life. Expressing gratitude not only deepens your connections but also reinforces your positive mindset.

Be gentle with yourself as you navigate the emotions and challenges of divorce. Cultivate gratitude for your strength, resilience, and ability to persevere. Acknowledge your efforts and progress, no matter how small it may seem, and celebrate your personal growth.

Remember, cultivating a gratitude practice during your divorce is a journey. Some days may be more challenging than others, but even amid difficulties, there are always moments of gratitude. By consciously practising gratitude, you can shift your focus, find joy in the present, and nurture a positive mindset that supports your well-being throughout the divorce process.

Remember, maintaining a positive attitude during a divorce is a journey that requires effort and self-compassion. You can navigate the challenges with resilience and grace by implementing these practical tips and finding what works best.

Let's move on to the next chapter and learn about key people who can help you go through your divorce gracefully and as effortlessly as possible.

Chapter 7:

Helpful People

Divorce can be overwhelming and emotionally challenging, leaving you feeling lost and uncertain about the future. While the support of family and friends is invaluable during this time, there is something uniquely valuable about the guidance and expertise of professionals. This chapter will explore the significance of working with legal, financial, and counselling professionals as you navigate the complex terrain of divorce. Though your loved ones offer immeasurable support, their perspectives may be coloured by their emotional involvement. Therefore, seeking the independent viewpoint of a professional can provide you with the clarity and objectivity necessary to make informed decisions and embark on a new chapter of your life.

Let's look at the different kinds of assistance you need to seek when going through a divorce.

SEEKING FINANCIAL ADVICE

When navigating the financial complexities of divorce, seek advice from professionals specialising in divorce-related financial matters. One of these professionals is a *Certified Public Accountant (CPA)* or *Certified Accountant (CA)*, who can help you with tax implications, asset division, and optimising your financial situation. You can also consult a *Financial Planner* or *Financial Advisor* to assist in analysing your finances, property division, financial support, and budgeting for a comprehensive plan. In some jurisdictions, you can get the help of a *Certified Divorce Financial Analyst (CDFA)*, who provides expertise on settlement options, asset assessment, retirement plans, and future financial projections. As you make your choices, seek referrals and conduct interviews to find the right fit.

Seeking professional financial advice is crucial for a variety of reasons. Let's explore the key points to understand why you need professional financial advice during this challenging time:

1. Understanding What You Have

As discussed in Chapter 3, a professional financial advisor can help you accurately assess your current financial situation. They will work with you to gather and organise all the necessary financial information, including assets, debts, income, and expenses. This comprehensive understanding of your financial position will enable you to make informed decisions about property division, spousal support, and child support.

For example, if you and your spouse own multiple properties, have investments, and hold joint accounts, a financial advisor can help you determine the value of these assets and provide guidance on how to distribute them equitably, considering tax implications and long-term financial considerations.

2. Managing Your Budget

Transitioning from one household to two can significantly impact your financial circumstances. A financial advisor can help you create a post-divorce budget that reflects your new reality. They will assist you in identifying essential expenses, prioritising financial obligations, and planning for future goals.

Consider a scenario where your income will decrease after the divorce, but you still need to maintain a certain standard of living for yourself and your children. A financial advisor can analyse your income and expenses, suggest areas for potential cost-cutting, and help you develop a budget that allows you to manage your finances effectively.

3. Adapting to One Home Becoming Two

Divorce often involves the division of shared assets, including the family home. A financial advisor can provide valuable guidance if you are transitioning to being a single homeowner or looking for a new place to live. They can help you assess the affordability of different housing options, evaluate mortgage options, and consider the long-term financial implications of your decisions.

For instance, you must decide whether to keep the family home or sell it and downsize. A financial advisor can help you analyse the financial impact of either choice, considering factors such as mortgage payments, property taxes, maintenance costs, and potential future appreciation.

4. Setting Realistic Financial Goals

Setting realistic financial goals that align with your new circumstances is essential during a divorce. A financial advisor can assist you in defining your short-term and long-term objectives, such as saving for retirement, funding education for your children, or establishing an emergency fund. They will consider your income, expenses, assets, and any potential financial support you may receive.

For example, suppose you have dreams of starting a new business after the divorce. In that case, a financial advisor can help you evaluate the feasibility of this goal and create a financial plan that supports your aspirations while ensuring financial stability.

5. Evaluating the Tax Implications

Divorce can have significant tax implications that may impact your financial situation in the short and long term. A financial advisor or accountant can help you understand the tax consequences of various financial decisions, such as the division of assets, spousal support, and child support. They can guide strategies to minimise tax liabilities and maximise your post-divorce financial position.

Suppose you are considering selling certain assets as part of the property division. In that case, an accountant can help you assess the potential capital gains taxes and explore options to optimise your tax position.

6. Planning for Retirement

Divorce can profoundly affect your retirement plans and financial security in your later years. A financial advisor can analyse your retirement savings (superannuation), pensions, and other assets to determine how the divorce may impact your retirement income. They can guide you in adjusting your retirement plans, making necessary modifications to ensure financial stability during your post-divorce years.

For instance, if you were relying on your spouse's pension for retirement income, a financial advisor can help you explore alternative retirement savings options and assist in developing a strategy to secure your financial future.

7. Addressing Financial Complexities

Divorce often involves complex financial matters, especially in high-net-worth cases or when business interests are involved. A financial advisor or accountant can help you navigate tricky financial situations, such as valuing and dividing businesses, assessing complex investment portfolios, or handling hidden assets. They can work alongside your lawyer to understand your financial landscape comprehensively and advocate for your best interests.

Suppose you and your spouse own a business together. In that case, a financial advisor or accountant can assist in determining the value of the business, negotiating a fair buyout or settlement, and providing recommendations on how to protect your financial interests.

8. Post-divorce Financial Planning

After the divorce is finalised, your financial situation will continue to evolve. A financial advisor can help you develop a long-term financial plan that reflects your new circumstances and goals. They can assist in optimising your investments, monitoring your cash flow, and adjusting your financial strategies as needed.

For instance, if you receive a lump sum settlement as part of the divorce, a financial advisor can guide you on investing or allocating those funds wisely, considering your risk tolerance, time frame, and financial objectives.

By working with a financial advisor, you can confidently navigate the financial complexities of divorce and make informed decisions that safeguard your financial well-being.

SEEKING LEGAL ADVICE

When going through a divorce, seeking legal advice from a qualified lawyer specialising in family law and divorce is essential. A lawyer focusing primarily on family law will have in-depth knowledge of the local laws, court procedures, and relevant precedents. This expertise ensures you receive accurate and practical legal guidance tailored to your situation. For instance, if you are going through a divorce involving disputes about where the children live, property division, and spousal support, an experienced family lawyer can navigate the intricacies of your jurisdiction's laws and advocate for the most favourable outcomes.

The lawyer will also assist you with the following:

1. Understanding the Dos and Don'ts of Separation

Early in the divorce process, your lawyer can provide vital guidance on the dos and don'ts of separation. They will advise you on protecting yourself legally and financially, ensuring you make informed decisions and safeguarding your interests. This may include guidance on issues such as communication with your spouse, asset preservation, and arrangements for children.

For example, your lawyer may advise you to communicate clearly and respectfully with your spouse to avoid misinterpretations or potential legal conflicts. They can also advise you on what actions to avoid, such as draining joint bank accounts or disposing of marital assets without proper legal procedures.

2. Developing a Strategic Approach

A skilled family lawyer can help you develop a strategic approach to your divorce. They will assess your unique circumstances, listen to your goals, and work with you to create a plan that aligns with your objectives. This may involve exploring negotiation or mediation options, preparing for litigation if necessary, or identifying potential areas of compromise.

Consider a situation where you and your spouse disagree on property division. A lawyer experienced in family law can help you evaluate the assets, assess their value, and develop a negotiation strategy that considers the relevant legal principles and maximises your outcome.

3. Preliminary Chat and Plan Development

Even if you are unsure about proceeding with a divorce, consulting with a lawyer for a preliminary chat can be highly beneficial. During this initial consultation, you can discuss your concerns, ask questions, and better understand your legal rights and options. This process allows you to make informed decisions about moving forward and empowers you to take control of your situation.

For instance, if you are uncertain about initiating a divorce or exploring reconciliation, a lawyer can provide an overview of the legal process, potential outcomes, and the steps involved. This preliminary chat can help you gather the necessary information to decide your next step.

4. Legal Knowledge and Documentation

A family lawyer possesses extensive legal knowledge and expertise in divorce-related matters. They can guide you through the legal process, ensuring you understand your rights, obligations, and the necessary documentation. They will assist you in completing and filing all required forms accurately and promptly, minimising the risk of errors or omissions that could delay your divorce proceedings.

For example, when drafting a comprehensive settlement agreement, your lawyer will address all crucial aspects, such as arrangements for the children, child support, spousal support, division of assets and debts, and other relevant provisions. They will work to protect your interests and advocate for fair and favourable terms in the agreement.

5. Mediation and Negotiation Support

If you and your spouse choose to work towards resolving your divorce through mediation or negotiation, your lawyer is vital in providing support and guidance. They will help you understand the potential outcomes, assess the proposed agreements in the context of the law in your jurisdiction, and advise you on the best course of action.

For instance, during mediation sessions, your lawyer can accompany you and guide you on what to expect, how to effectively communicate your needs and concerns, and evaluate the proposed agreements to ensure they are in your best interest.

6. Court Representation

In cases where litigation becomes necessary, having a lawyer by your side is crucial. They will represent your interests in court, present your case effectively, and advocate for your rights before the judge. Your lawyer will prepare legal arguments, gather evidence, cross-examine witnesses, and offer a compelling case on your behalf.

Where there is a dispute over where the children live or how they spend time with the other parent, your lawyer will help you consider evidence, talk to experts, and present a strong case to demonstrate your ability to provide your children with a stable and loving environment. They will advocate for an arrangement that prioritises the children's best interests.

7. Knowledge of Alternative Dispute Resolution Methods

Apart from traditional litigation, alternative dispute resolution methods such as collaborative divorce or arbitration may be suitable for your situation. A family lawyer can explain these options, assess their appropriateness, and guide you in choosing the most effective approach for resolving your divorce.

If you and your spouse are committed to maintaining an amicable relationship and reaching a mutually beneficial agreement, your lawyer can advise you on the collaborative divorce process. They will help assemble a team of professionals, including financial specialists and counsellors, to facilitate negotiations and foster a cooperative atmosphere.

By seeking legal advice from a family lawyer, you can benefit from their expertise, understand the dos and don'ts of separation, develop a strategic approach to your divorce, and gain clarity through a preliminary chat. Remember, a knowledgeable lawyer will provide the guidance and advocacy necessary to advocate for your interests, navigate the legal complexities, and achieve the best possible outcome in your divorce.

SEEKING HELP FROM A PROFESSIONAL COUNSELLOR OR THERAPIST

As you have read earlier in this book, divorce can be an emotional rollercoaster, and having the assistance of a professional therapist or counsellor can be immensely valuable throughout the process. Even if you feel confident in your decision and believe you are handling the situation well, divorce often triggers complex emotions and challenges that can be better managed with professional support. It is essential to recognise that divorce involves a grief process, and working with a therapist can provide the guidance and tools needed to navigate this journey effectively. Additionally, professionals understand that individuals process their emotions differently and have the expertise to address various situations.

Working with a professional therapist or counsellor during your divorce will help you in the following ways:

1. Emotional Support and Coping Strategies

A therapist or counsellor can provide a safe and non-judgmental space in which you can express your feelings, fears, and concerns during this challenging time. They offer emotional support and help you develop healthy coping strategies to navigate the ups and downs of the divorce process. Working with a professional can help you to gain insights into your emotions, learn effective stress management techniques, and cultivate resilience.

If you find yourself experiencing intense anger or sadness, a therapist can help you explore the underlying causes, provide tools to manage these emotions constructively, and guide you in developing self-care practices to promote emotional well-being.

2. Managing Co-parenting and Communication Challenges

Divorce often involves ongoing co-parenting and communication with your ex-spouse. A therapist or counsellor can assist you in navigating the complexities of this relationship and developing effective strategies for healthy communication and co-parenting.

Consider a situation where you and your ex-spouse have different parenting styles and struggle to agree on the children's upbringing. A therapist can help facilitate communication, offer guidance on setting boundaries, and provide techniques to foster cooperation and respectful co-parenting.

3. Building Resilience and Personal Growth

Divorce presents an opportunity for personal growth and transformation. A therapist can support you in identifying and embracing this opportunity by helping you to reflect on the lessons learned and explore your personal values and goals, facilitating your journey toward healing and resilience.

Suppose you find it challenging to release negative emotions or move forward after the divorce. In that case, a therapist can assist you in processing these feelings, reframing your perspective and helping you to create a positive mindset for the future.

4. Navigating the Grief Process

As discussed earlier, divorce often involves a grieving process similar to the one that occurs with other significant losses in life. A therapist or counsellor can guide you through this process, helping you understand and accept the stages of grief, such as denial, anger, bargaining, depression, and acceptance. They can provide coping strategies for grief-related emotions, such as sadness, loneliness, and feelings of loss.

For example, if you struggle with guilt or loss of identity after the divorce, a therapist can help you work through these emotions, challenge any self-blame, and support you in finding a renewed sense of self.

5. Tailored Support for Your Individual Needs

Every divorce is different, and a professional therapist or counsellor recognises this. They have the knowledge and skills to adapt their approach to your specific circumstances and individual needs. They can address anxiety, depression, self-esteem issues, and trauma related to the divorce, providing customised support that fosters your emotional well-being.

If you experienced emotional abuse during your marriage, a therapist can help you navigate the healing process, rebuild your self-esteem, and establish healthy boundaries in your post-divorce life.

6. Managing Stress and Anxiety

Significant levels of stress and anxiety often accompany divorce. A therapist or counsellor can help you identify and manage stress triggers, develop effective relaxation techniques, and provide strategies to reduce anxiety. They can guide self-care practices and stress reduction exercises to promote well-being during this challenging time.

The legal complexities of divorce can be overwhelming for some people. A therapist can teach stress management techniques such as deep breathing exercises, mindfulness practices, or guided imagery to help you find calm and maintain emotional balance.

7. Creating a Support Network

Going through a divorce can feel isolating and lonely. A therapist or counsellor can help you build a support network beyond friends and family. They can connect you with divorce support groups, community resources, or other professionals specialising in divorce-related issues. This network can provide valuable insights, empathy, and a sense of community, helping you navigate the challenges of divorce more effectively.

A therapist may recommend joining a divorce support group where you can connect with others who are going through similar experiences. Being part of such a group can provide validation, shared experiences, and practical advice, fostering a sense of belonging and support. Be wary of a support group whose primary purpose is negative or rights-based (advocating for the rights of a particular group). Find an inclusive group to take in a balanced perspective.

8. Child-focused Guidance

If you have children, a therapist or counsellor can guide you in how to support them through the divorce process. They can help you understand the impact of divorce on children at different developmental stages, offer strategies for effective co-parenting, and assist in addressing any emotional or behavioural challenges your children may experience.

A therapist can help you develop age-appropriate explanations about the divorce for your children, facilitate open and honest communication, and support them in expressing their emotions and adjusting to the new family dynamic.

9. Healing and Closure

Divorce can leave emotional wounds that require healing and closure. A therapist or counsellor can guide you through this healing process, allowing you to work through unresolved emotions, let go of any lingering pain or resentment, and move forward with a renewed sense of self and purpose.

If you are struggling with forgiveness or finding it challenging to envision a positive future after the divorce, a therapist can provide a safe and supportive space to explore these emotions, process any unresolved issues, and help you find the inner strength to embrace a new chapter in your life.

A professional counsellor or therapist will make your divorce journey less stressful by giving you valuable advice and practical coping strategies so that you can shift your perspective and gracefully get through this difficult time.

KEY POINTS TO REMEMBER WHEN SEEKING HELP

Here are some things you need to keep in mind even as you seek help through this tough time:

One of the most crucial steps you can take when going through a divorce is to **seek professional advice early in the process**. By doing so, you set yourself up strategically and gain a clear understanding of the path ahead. Seeking financial, legal, and counselling advice will help you address the unknowns, avoid making hasty or irrational mistakes, and make informed decisions. Early advice can lay a solid foundation for your divorce proceedings and empower you to navigate the complexities of the process with confidence.

While your friends and family undoubtedly have your best interests at heart, it's essential to understand that their emotions and personal experiences may influence their advice. While their support is invaluable, relying solely on their guidance may not provide the objective viewpoint you need during this critical time. **Seeking the input of professionals who can offer an impartial and unbiased perspective is essential**. They can help you see beyond your emotions and provide guidance based on their expertise and experience, ensuring your decisions are grounded in sound judgment.

It is important to remember that no two divorces are the same. **Each individual's circumstances, dynamics, and needs are unique,** and your divorce should be approached in a way that respects and reflects your distinct situation. Professionals in divorce understand this and can tailor their advice and support to meet your needs. They will work with you to develop a personalised strategy that considers your unique circumstances, helping you navigate the complexities of the divorce process in a way best suited for your situation.

By keeping these essential points in mind, you can approach seeking help during your divorce with clarity and purpose. Remember, early advice, an independent perspective, and an appreciation for your individuality will contribute to a smoother and more informed journey through this challenging chapter of your life.

Let's move on to the next chapter and get more tips on navigating divorce.

Chapter 8:

Rules to Live By

Amid the emotional turmoil accompanying divorce, you must be gracious as you navigate this challenging chapter of life. While every situation is unique and advice may vary, there are three steadfast rules to live by that can help you stay afloat even when your world is crumbling. This chapter will explore these guiding principles that can provide solace and clarity amidst chaos. By embracing these rules and applying them to your journey, you can find a sense of stability and empowerment, even when faced with the toughest of circumstances. So, please take a deep breath, hold onto hope, and let's discover the unwavering rules that can guide you through the storm of divorce.

RULE 1: ALWAYS DO THE RIGHT THING

When going through a divorce, always doing the right thing means consistently acting with integrity and making fair, honest, and respectful decisions. It entails upholding moral principles and ethical standards throughout the divorce, even when faced with difficult emotions or circumstances. Doing the right thing means prioritising fairness, transparency, open communication, and seeking mutually beneficial resolutions whenever possible. By always doing the right thing, you demonstrate a commitment to integrity and uphold your values, regardless of the actions or behaviours of others. It means taking the high road and refraining from vindictiveness, manipulation, or revenge. Instead, you approach conflicts with empathy, understanding, and a willingness to find common ground.

Doing the right thing during a divorce looks like this.

Maintaining **open and honest communication** with your ex-spouse is essential. Respectfully express your needs, concerns, and expectations and actively listen to other perspectives. For example, if you need to discuss arrangements for the children, approach the conversation with a willingness to compromise and find a solution that prioritises the well-being of your children.

Ensuring a *division of assets and debts that accords with the legal principles in your jurisdiction is crucial* during a divorce. Remember, it may not always seem or feel fair. Disclose all relevant financial information and work together to reach a reasonable settlement. For instance, if you discover a hidden bank account or asset, disclosing it and including it in the division process is essential, even if it may not be in your immediate financial interest.

Putting the best interests of your children first is a vital aspect of doing the right thing during a divorce. Maintain a positive co-parenting relationship and foster a supportive environment for your children by, for example, encouraging and supporting their relationship with the other parent, attending their important events together, and facilitating open and honest communication between all parties involved.

Respecting each other's boundaries and privacy is crucial. Refrain from invading personal space, accessing private information without consent, or using sensitive information as leverage. For instance, avoid the temptation to snoop through personal emails or messages, as it violates trust and can escalate conflicts unnecessarily.

Approaching conflicts or disagreements with a *collaborative mindset* is essential. Seek mutually beneficial solutions and consider the long-term implications of decisions. For example, if there is a disagreement about property division, explore mediation or involve professionals to help facilitate a fair resolution.

Adhering to legal obligations and following court orders is essential to do the right thing. Respect the legal process, attend court hearings, and fulfil financial obligations like child support or alimony and support payments. For instance, consistently make timely and accurate financial contributions as stipulated by the court, even if circumstances change or disagreements arise.

Shielding children from unnecessary conflict and maintaining a peaceful environment is crucial. Avoid heated arguments or negative conversations about the other parent in the presence of the children. Refrain from speaking negatively about your ex-spouse during exchanges, and ensure children are not put in the position of being messengers between parents.

Respecting and honouring agreed parenting schedules is essential for fostering stability and predictability for children. It means punctuality and reliability with drop-offs, pick-ups, and visitation times. For instance, consistently adhere to the agreed-upon schedule and provide ample notice for necessary modifications.

Recognising the **value of professional guidance and seeking it when necessary** is a responsible choice. Consult with legal, financial, or mental health professionals to navigate complex issues or disputes. Involve a mediator to help facilitate discussions or enlist the expertise of a financial advisor to ensure a fair division of assets.

Respecting the confidentiality of sensitive information shared during the divorce process is vital. Refrain from discussing intimate details or airing grievances publicly or on social media platforms. Avoid posting derogatory comments or private information about your ex-spouse on social media, as it can further cause unnecessary harm and strain relationships.

Where it is safe and appropriate to do so, **encouraging and supporting a positive relationship between children and the other parent** demonstrates a commitment to their well-being. Refrain from interfering or attempting to alienate the children from the other parent. Facilitate regular communication, share important updates and photographs, and encourage children to maintain a healthy and loving relationship with both parents.

Taking care of your well-being and seeking emotional support during a divorce is crucial. Acknowledge and process your emotions healthily, seek professional help, or lean on a support system when needed. Engage in self-care activities, such as therapy, exercise, or hobbies, to help manage stress and maintain your emotional balance.

Incorporating these principles into your actions and decisions demonstrates a commitment to doing the right thing during your divorce. It may not always be easy, but by approaching conflicts with integrity, respect, and a focus on fairness, you can navigate the divorce process to uphold your values and promote a healthier and more peaceful transition for everyone involved.

RULE 2: DON'T REACT, ACT

During the challenging divorce process, you must shift your focus from reacting to acting. When your partner engages in behaviours that may upset or provoke you, reacting impulsively or reciprocating with negative actions is tempting. However, you maintain your integrity and rise above the situation by acting instead of reacting. Rather than stooping to their level, take a step back, allow yourself to calm down, and address the issues non-reactively. Doing so lets you regain control over your emotions and responses, ensuring that your decisions are driven by reason and fairness. Remember, in these moments of composure and thoughtful action, you can navigate the complexities of divorce with grace and preserve your self-respect.

How do you do that, you may wonder? Here are practical tips on how to avoid reacting and instead focus on acting even as you go through your divorce.

Pausing at stages of your divorce process is a powerful tool that allows you to regain control over your emotions and respond to challenging situations with greater clarity and composure. It involves permitting yourself to step back, take a deep breath, and create a space between the trigger and your response. It may not be possible if there are pressing deadlines, but a pause can be as simple as going for a walk, having a coffee by the beach for an hour, or reading a book. Anything that gives your mind a break to reset and keep going.

When emotions run high during a divorce, it's easy to get caught up in the heat of the moment and react impulsively. Pausing enables you to regain your composure and avoid saying or doing something you might regret later. If your ex-spouse sends a provocative text message, pausing allows you to create a buffer between the emotional trigger and your response, giving you time to collect your thoughts and respond more calmly.

By stepping away from a situation momentarily, you create space for clarity and perspective. This pause allows you to reflect on the situation objectively, consider the consequences of your actions, and make a more informed decision on how to respond. For example, suppose you receive a challenging email from your ex-spouse filled with accusations. In that case, pausing allows you to assess the situation, consult trusted advisors if needed, and respond to your long-term goals.

Remember, pausing is not a sign of weakness but rather an act of self-care and emotional intelligence. It allows you to navigate challenging moments with greater control and intention, ensuring that your actions align with your values and desired outcomes. The pause can be as short as a few moments or as long as needed to regain balance. Incorporating this practice into your divorce journey can foster healthier communication, help you to make more thoughtful decisions, and contribute to a more peaceful and constructive process.

Practising active listening during a divorce is a crucial skill that fosters effective communication and promotes a more respectful and productive dialogue. It involves giving full attention to the other person without prematurely interrupting or formulating your response.

Active listening allows you to understand the other person's perspective genuinely. You can fully grasp their concerns, needs, and emotions by giving them your undivided attention. Listening actively lets you hear their worries, desires, and motivations without immediately interjecting with your agenda when discussing parenting arrangements with your ex-spouse.

Understanding their perspective creates a foundation for finding common ground and developing solutions that meet both parties' needs. By actively listening, you demonstrate empathy and respect for the other person's point of view. It shows that you value their opinions and are willing to engage in constructive dialogue. Instead of reacting defensively or dismissively, you can respond more thoughtfully. For instance, when your ex-spouse expresses concerns about arrangements for the children to spend time with them, active listening allows you to respond with empathy, address their worries, and acknowledge their perspective while still advocating for your needs.

Practising active listening requires patience and self-awareness. It involves temporarily setting aside your agenda to hear and understand genuinely the other person's thoughts and feelings. Active listening can contribute to healthier interactions, improved problem-solving, and a more harmonious resolution during a divorce by fostering an open and attentive communication climate.

Engage the services of a mediator, counsellor, or family therapist who can provide guidance and facilitate productive communication. *A neutral third party can create a safe space for both parties to express their feelings and concerns*, reducing the likelihood of reactive behaviours. For example, if you and your ex-spouse are struggling to compromise on the arrangements for the children, a family therapist can assist in finding a fair solution that takes into account the children's needs, ages, and stages of development and, hopefully, satisfies both parties.

When addressing an issue, **respond in a manner that is respectful yet assertive**. Clearly express your concerns or boundaries while avoiding personal attacks or blame. If your ex-spouse repeatedly fails to adhere to parenting schedules, calmly address the issue by stating your expectations and proposing potential solutions to ensure smoother transitions for your children.

Consult with your lawyer or other legal professionals to clarify your rights and responsibilities. This knowledge empowers you to make informed decisions and respond effectively to any legal challenges that may arise. For example, if your ex-spouse threatens to withhold financial support, consult your lawyer to understand your options and take appropriate action.

Prioritise self-care to maintain your emotional well-being throughout the divorce process. Engage in activities that reduce stress and promote a positive mindset, such as exercise, meditation, or spending time with supportive friends and family. By taking care of yourself, you enhance your ability to respond thoughtfully instead of reacting impulsively.

Focus on the bigger picture and the long-term outcomes you desire from the divorce. Remind yourself of your goals and the life you envision beyond the divorce. This perspective can help you stay grounded and make decisions that align with your future well-being. For example, if your ex-spouse tries to engage in a contentious argument during a negotiation session, remind yourself of your goal to reach a fair settlement and consider how engaging in that argument may impact that outcome.

Use journaling as a tool to express and process your emotions healthily. Writing down your thoughts and feelings can provide a release and help you gain clarity before responding to challenging situations. For example, if you receive an aggressive email from your ex-spouse, take a moment to write down your initial reactions in your journal. This practice lets you process your emotions privately and respond later with a more composed and constructive message.

Cultivate empathy and compassion for yourself and your ex-spouse throughout the divorce process. Recognise that both of you may be experiencing emotional challenges and approach interactions with understanding and kindness. You create an environment that promotes more respectful and productive communication by fostering empathy. If your ex-spouse expresses frustrations or concerns, listen with empathy and respond in a way that acknowledges their feelings while still asserting your needs.

Remember, you retain control over your actions and emotions during the divorce process by choosing to act rather than react. While it may be challenging at times, practising these tips can help you navigate difficult situations in a way that upholds your integrity and contributes to a more constructive and respectful resolution.

RULE 3: PICK YOUR BATTLES

During the tumultuous journey of divorce, you must understand the significance of picking and choosing your battles wisely. Throughout this process, you may encounter criticism, opinions, and even confrontations from your ex-partner, mutual friends, and family members. However, it would be best to recognise that you cannot engage in every argument or justify yourself to everyone. Instead, focus on preserving your emotional well-being and directing your energy toward battles that truly matter.

By selectively engaging in battles, you can prioritise what truly deserves your attention. Not every disagreement or criticism warrants your immediate response or validation. Take a step back, breathe, and evaluate the situation objectively. Ask yourself, *"Does this issue align with my long-term goals? Will it significantly impact my well-being or that of my children?"* By asking these questions, you understand which battles are worth your time and energy.

Remember, you are not obligated to justify your decisions or defend yourself to everyone who questions or criticises you. Focus on maintaining your sense of integrity and well-being. As Buddha wisely said, *"You will not be punished for your anger; your anger will punish you."* Choose battles that align with your values and bring you closer to a positive resolution. By doing so, you reclaim your power and create a path that leads to a happier future beyond the turmoil of divorce.

Here are some practical tips on picking your battles wisely and preserving your energy for the things that truly matter.

Take the time to **define your priorities and long-term goals clearly**. By understanding what matters most to you, you can focus your energy on battles that align with those priorities. If co-parenting your children in a healthy and supportive manner is a top priority, you may let go of minor disagreements about personal possessions and instead invest your energy in establishing a solid co-parenting plan.

Evaluate the potential impact of engaging in a particular battle. Consider the emotional toll, financial cost, and possible long-term consequences of getting involved. Ask yourself if the issue at hand is worth the potential negative impacts it may bring. If your ex-spouse insists on a specific furniture item during the division of assets, weigh the importance of that item against the potential stress and legal fees that may arise from fighting over it.

Consult with your lawyer, therapist, or other trusted advisors who can provide objective guidance. They can help you assess the importance of various battles and provide insight into the potential outcomes. If you are uncertain about contesting a particular aspect of the divorce settlement, seek your lawyer's advice to understand the potential benefits and drawbacks before deciding.

Practising emotional detachment during a divorce is crucial for maintaining your well-being and making sound decisions. It involves stepping back from unnecessary conflicts and provocations and allowing yourself to respond thoughtfully rather than impulsively. By doing so, you can avoid being drawn into heated arguments that may only prolong the pain and hinder the healing process.

Here's a deeper exploration of the importance of emotional detachment and how it can be applied in real-life situations:

- **Preserving your well-being**: Emotional detachment allows you to protect your emotional well-being during a divorce. It means recognising that engaging in every argument or confrontation will drain your energy and prolong the healing process. If your ex-spouse makes hurtful remarks about your character or tries to provoke you, practising emotional detachment can help you maintain your self-esteem and emotional stability, preventing their words or actions from negatively affecting you.
- **Prioritising your children's well-being**: Emotional detachment is especially crucial when children are involved. It allows you to prioritise their well-being above all else. Instead of engaging in confrontations that may harm your children's perception of the situation or create tension, you can respond calmly and neutrally. If your ex-spouse attempts to instigate an argument during an exchange of your children, practising emotional detachment enables you to prioritise your children's stability and maintain a peaceful environment.

Focus on the bigger picture and the desired outcome of a peaceful and fair resolution. Remind yourself that engaging in every battle may hinder your ability to achieve a positive outcome and move forward with your life. Suppose your ex-spouse engages in a smear campaign against you with mutual friends. In that case, you may prioritise your personal growth and well-being rather than investing time and energy in defending yourself against every rumour.

Consider the likelihood of resolving the issue in a particular battle. Suppose the issue is highly contentious, and the chances of finding a mutually agreeable solution are low. In that case, ***focusing on matters with a higher probability of reaching a satisfactory outcome may be more beneficial***. For example, if negotiating parenting arrangements with your ex-spouse has consistently led to impasses, prioritise working on aspects of the property distribution if that is less contentious and try to reach an agreement.

Be mindful of the battles that significantly negatively impact your mental and emotional health. Doing away with conflicts that continuously drain your energy and cause unnecessary distress may be necessary. If engaging in a particular argument triggers intense emotional turmoil and affects your ability to function, it may be best to disengage and focus on self-care instead.

Reflect on the long-term effects of an ongoing dispute on your relationships, especially if you have children. Engaging in constant conflict with your ex-spouse can create a hostile environment and strain relationships with your children. Choose battles, prioritising maintaining a healthy co-parenting dynamic and fostering positive relationships with your children. Instead of arguing about minor scheduling conflicts, focus on building a solid foundation of communication and cooperation for the well-being of your children.

Trust your intuition and listen to your inner voice when deciding which disputes to engage in. Your instincts can provide valuable guidance on what is truly important to you and what battles align with your values and principles. While seeking advice from professionals and trusted advisors is essential, ultimately, you know your situation best. Trust yourself to make decisions that will serve your best interests and lead to a more positive post-divorce future.

By implementing these practical tips, you can navigate the complexities of your divorce with greater clarity and choose battles that truly matter. Remember, picking your fights allows you to protect your well-being, maintain your focus on long-term goals, and pave the way for a smoother transition into the next chapter of your life. After going through the divorce, your life must go on.

Let's move on to the next chapter and examine how you can create a beautiful life even after a difficult divorce.

Chapter 9:

The Future Is Yours

Congratulations! You've embarked on a new chapter of your life and a fresh start, full of infinite possibilities. Divorce may have marked the end of your partnership, but it also signifies the beginning of a remarkable journey of self-discovery and personal growth. In this chapter, we will explore the incredible potential that lies ahead of you. It's time to reclaim your identity, embrace your individuality, and create a life that is uniquely yours.

Divorce can be an emotional rollercoaster, filled with uncertainty, grief, and the need to rebuild. But amidst the turbulence, an exciting truth awaits you: you have the power to craft a future that is even more fulfilling and joyful than you ever imagined. It's time to rediscover the essence of who you are and reignite the passions that may have been overshadowed during your previous chapter.

FINDING HAPPINESS AND JOY AFTER DIVORCE

Finding happiness even after a divorce brings numerous benefits that can positively impact every aspect of your life. Firstly, being happy allows you to heal and move forward from the emotional pain and challenges of the divorce. It gives you the strength and resilience to embrace your new reality and create a fulfilling life. Happiness enhances your overall mental and physical well-being, promoting better health and a higher quality of life. It allows you to let go of bitterness and resentment, freeing yourself from negative emotions that can weigh you down.

When you're happy, you radiate positivity and attract positive experiences and people. It opens the door to new opportunities, relationships, and personal growth. Furthermore, finding happiness after a divorce sets a powerful example for your children, showing them that life goes on and they, too, can find happiness despite their challenges.

Things to Do to Regain Your Happiness and Joy

I know you want to be happy again, and you probably wonder what you must do to feel alive and bubbly again. Well, here are some tips:

Prioritise your physical, emotional, and mental well-being. Engage in activities that nurture and rejuvenate you, such as exercise, meditation, getting enough sleep, and maintaining a healthy diet. Taking care of yourself holistically can boost your mood, increase your energy levels, and enhance your overall well-being.

Take this opportunity to reflect on your values, aspirations, and dreams. *Set meaningful goals for yourself and work towards them.* Whether pursuing a new career path, furthering your education, or embarking on a personal development journey, investing in your growth can empower you and bring a sense of purpose and fulfilment.

After a divorce, it's essential to *recognise that not everyone will fully understand or empathise with your experience.* Divorce is a deeply personal and complex journey, and each individual's circumstances are unique. While seeking support and validation from others is natural, it's crucial to understand that not everyone can comprehend the full extent of what you've been through.

This understanding can contribute to your happiness after divorce by relieving the pressure to seek approval or understanding from others. It allows you to focus on your healing and personal growth without constantly seeking validation from external sources. When you embrace that not everyone will understand, you can let go of the need to justify or explain yourself to those unable to relate.

By accepting that not everyone will understand, you free yourself from the burden of trying to please or gain approval from others. This empowers you to prioritise your well-being and happiness. Instead of seeking validation externally, you can turn inward and focus on self-care, personal development, and nurturing relationships with those who support and understand you.

Develop a mindset of thankfulness by *recognising the positive aspects of your life* and focusing on what you have rather than what you have lost. Incorporate gratitude practices into your daily routine, such as keeping a gratitude journal or expressing appreciation for the small things. Additionally, practise positive self-talk and challenge negative thoughts or self-limiting beliefs that may arise during this transition.

Step out of your comfort zone and *embrace new experiences*. Travel to new places, try different cuisines, or engage in activities that challenge and inspire you. Opening yourself up to new possibilities can broaden your perspective, boost your confidence, and bring a sense of excitement and adventure into your life.

Take control of your life and *make decisions that align with your values and aspirations*. Set boundaries that protect your emotional well-being and prioritise your needs. Embrace your independence and learn to rely on yourself for happiness and fulfilment. You'll feel renewed confidence and self-worth as you assert your autonomy and reclaim your power.

Consider *seeking guidance from a therapist, counsellor, or life coach* specialising in divorce recovery. Professional support can provide valuable tools, coping strategies, and insights to help you navigate emotional challenges and build a resilient mindset. A skilled professional can offer personalised guidance tailored to your needs and circumstances.

Volunteering or helping others in need can be incredibly rewarding and uplifting. *Engaging in acts of kindness* benefits others and allows you to shift your focus away from your challenges and find fulfilment in positively impacting someone else's life. It can bring a sense of purpose, gratitude, and connection with your community.

Use this transitional phase to explore and rediscover yourself. ***Engage in self-reflection, journaling, or mindfulness practices to better understand your values, desires, and aspirations.*** Practise self-love and self-compassion by treating yourself with kindness, forgiveness, and acceptance. Cultivate a loving relationship with yourself, honouring your strengths and embracing your uniqueness.

Remember, regaining happiness after a divorce is a personal journey that takes time and self-compassion. Be patient with yourself, celebrate your progress, and seek support when needed. By focusing on self-care, rediscovering your passions, fostering connections, embracing personal growth, and cultivating gratitude, you can reclaim your happiness and create a fulfilling life post-divorce.

MAKING NEW FRIENDS AFTER DIVORCE

Making new friends after a divorce is crucial for your emotional well-being and personal growth. While your old friends may have been a significant part of your life, some may have connections to your ex-spouse, which can be constant reminders of your past relationship. Moving on from a divorce requires a fresh start and building a new support network that aligns with your current journey.

Making new friends allows you to surround yourself with individuals who support your growth, understand your new life circumstances, and provide a fresh perspective. These new connections can bring excitement, new experiences, and a sense of belonging. While you don't necessarily have to cut off all your old friends, forging new friendships provides an opportunity to create a positive and supportive social circle that contributes to your healing process and helps you move forward with renewed optimism and joy.

How to Make New Friends

Here are some tips to help you make new friends after a divorce and embark on a fresh start:

Get involved in activities, groups, or communities that align with your interests and **expand your social circle**. Join clubs, classes, or hobby groups where you can meet like-minded individuals and connect with them over shared passions. For example, join a local hiking group or outdoor adventure club if you enjoy hiking.

Make an effort to **attend social events and gatherings** where you can meet new people. This can include parties, networking events, or even casual get-togethers with colleagues or acquaintances. Embrace these opportunities to introduce yourself, engage in conversations, and build new connections.

Find local **volunteer opportunities** that resonate with your values or interests. Volunteering allows you to contribute positively to your community and exposes you to like-minded individuals who share your passion for making a difference.

Utilise **online platforms** such as social media groups or specialised websites that connect people with similar hobbies or interests. These platforms provide a convenient way to connect with individuals seeking new friendships and social connections.

Approach new social situations with an **open mind and a friendly demeanour**. Smile, engage in conversations, and actively listen to others. Show genuine interest in getting to know people, and be open to forming new connections without carrying the baggage of your past.

Consider **enrolling in classes or workshops** that align with your interests or hobbies. Whether learning a new language, painting, or joining a fitness group, these activities provide opportunities to meet new people who share similar passions and create connections based on common interests.

Joining support groups specifically designed for individuals going through a divorce can be beneficial in connecting with others who understand your experiences. These groups provide a safe space in which to share your feelings, gain support, and form friendships with people on a similar journey.

Remember, building new friendships takes time and effort. Be patient with yourself and others, and don't be afraid to take the initiative in reaching out and organising social activities. Gradually, as you invest in these new connections, you'll find yourself surrounded by a supportive network of friends who will help you embrace your fresh start with enthusiasm and joy.

RECONNECTING WITH HOBBIES AND PASSION PROJECTS AFTER DIVORCE

Reconnecting with your hobbies and passion projects after divorce can be a transformative experience as you embark on a fresh start. Your hobbies and passions may have taken a backseat or were even forgotten during your marriage. Rediscovering and rekindling these flames can profoundly impact your well-being and overall happiness. Engaging in activities you genuinely enjoy and are passionate about allows you to reconnect with your authentic self, reclaim your identity, and foster personal growth.

By immersing yourself in your hobbies and passion projects, you permit yourself to prioritise your needs and desires. Whether it's painting, playing a musical instrument, writing, gardening, or any other activity that brings you joy, these pursuits provide an outlet for self-expression, creativity, and personal fulfilment. They remind you of your unique talents and abilities, boosting your confidence and self-esteem. Engaging with your hobbies allows you to experience a sense of accomplishment, growth, and satisfaction, which can be incredibly empowering as you navigate your new life post-divorce.

How to Reconnect With Your Hobbies and Passions

In case you're wondering where to begin with reconnecting with your hobbies and passions, here are some tips:

Reflect on the activities and interests that brought you joy before your marriage. Think about what you were passionate about and what activities made you feel alive. This self-reflection will help you identify the hobbies and passions that you want to reconnect with.

Begin by **taking small steps** to reintegrate your hobbies into your life. Set aside dedicated time each week to engage in your chosen activity, even if it's just for a short period. Starting small allows you to ease back into your hobbies without overwhelming yourself.

Use this opportunity to **explore new hobbies or activities** you've always been curious about. Consider trying something completely different from what you used to do. This exploration can spark new passions and open doors to exciting experiences.

Be patient and kind to yourself as you rediscover your hobbies. It's normal to feel rusty or out of practice at first. Embrace the learning process and allow yourself to grow and improve over time. Remember, the journey itself is just as important as the result.

Surround yourself with sources of inspiration related to your hobbies. This can include books, magazines, online forums, or social media groups focused on your interests. Engaging with inspiring content can reignite your passion and provide fresh ideas for your creative endeavours.

Creating a dedicated space in your home for your hobbies is a powerful way to cultivate a supportive and inspiring environment for reconnecting with your passions after a divorce. This space is a physical reminder of your commitment to self-care and personal growth and provides a haven to fully immerse yourself in your chosen activities.

A designated space for your hobbies visualises your intention to prioritise and invest in your happiness. It is a constant reminder that you deserve time and space to engage in activities that bring you joy and fulfilment. This dedicated space can act as a sanctuary where you can escape the stress and challenges of daily life, allowing you to focus on reconnecting with your passions and rekindling your sense of self.

The key is creating a space tailored to your specific hobbies and preferences. Consider the activities you enjoy and the materials or equipment you need. Whether it's a corner of a room, a spare bedroom, or even a dedicated studio space, ensure it is organised and free from distractions. Personalise the space with items that inspire and motivate you, such as artwork, photographs, or meaningful objects that ignite your creativity and enthusiasm.

Seek local clubs, groups, or communities that focus on your interests. Whether it's a book club, sports team, art class, or volunteer organisation, *joining like-minded individuals will provide a supportive and motivating environment* to reconnect with your passions.

Making your hobbies and passions a priority in your schedule is crucial for reconnecting with them after a divorce. It's easy to let life's demands and responsibilities take precedence, leaving little time for activities that bring you joy. By intentionally setting aside dedicated time slots for your hobbies, you ensure they receive the attention and respect they deserve.

Blocking out specific time slots in your schedule provides structure and ensures you won't overlook or dismiss your hobbies as mere indulgences. Treat these time slots as non-negotiable appointments with yourself, just like any other important commitment. This signals that your hobbies are just as important as any other obligation in your life.

Remember, reconnecting with your hobbies and passions is a personal journey. Be open to exploring new avenues, experimenting with different activities, and allowing yourself the freedom to enjoy the process. Embrace the joy and fulfilment of rediscovering your passions and let them guide you towards a fresh start after your divorce.

LEARNING TO TRUST AGAIN

Trust can feel like a fragile and distant memory after a divorce. The wounds of betrayal and heartache may leave you hesitant to open your heart to others, fearing that history may repeat itself. But amidst the pain and uncertainty, there is hope. Trust, like a delicate flower, can be nurtured and revived. It is a process of healing, growth, and self-discovery. Let's explore the intricacies of rebuilding trust within yourself, embracing vulnerability, and fostering authentic connections with others.

How to Trust Again After a Divorce

As impossible as it sounds, you can move on and learn to trust again despite your divorce. Here are some tips to guide you along this journey of rebuilding trust with yourself and with others:

Practising self-trust is an empowering journey of developing a deep connection with yourself. *It starts by reflecting on your values, strengths, and intuition*. When you take the time to understand what truly matters to you and recognise your unique capabilities, you lay the foundation for trusting your judgment and decision-making abilities. By listening to your inner voice, you gain valuable insights that can guide you toward choices aligned with your authentic self.

Permit yourself to heal from the wounds of the past. *It's essential to process your emotions, seek closure, and release any lingering resentments*.

This might involve seeking support from a therapist, journaling, or engaging in activities that promote self-care and emotional healing.

Take *small steps to rebuild trust* in your interactions with others. Start by opening up to close friends or family members who have demonstrated reliability and understanding. Gradually expand your circle of trust as you feel more comfortable and secure.

Honest and open communication is vital to rebuilding trust. *Share your feelings, concerns, and expectations with others*. Be transparent about your boundaries and needs, and encourage others to do the same. Clear and compassionate communication fosters understanding and helps build a solid trust foundation.

Remember that trust is not built overnight. *Allow yourself the time and space to rebuild trust at your own pace*. Be patient with yourself and others, and acknowledge that building trust is a gradual process.

While learning from the past is essential, *avoid projecting your past experiences onto new relationships*. Give each person a clean slate and an opportunity to prove themselves. Embrace the present moment and allow yourself to experience new connections without the weight of past disappointments.

Forgiveness is a powerful tool for healing and rebuilding trust. It doesn't mean forgetting or condoning the past. Rather, it is a way to free yourself from resentment and anger. Forgiving others and yourself allows you to move forward with an open heart.

Remember, learning to trust again is a personal journey, and everyone's timeline will differ. Be kind to yourself throughout the process and celebrate the milestones, no matter how small. Trust is a precious gift; rebuilding it will create the opportunity for deeper connections and a more fulfilling life.

Conclusion

So what have we learned along the way in this divorce-by-design journey?

The outcomes of your separation and divorce come down to choice, your choice.

Understanding how your *emotions* play a part in your divorce, knowing where you are in the *grief cycle* and understanding how your *personality* might impact how you manage the divorce process (the ups and downs in true rollercoaster form) allow you to make a conscious choice about what steps you will take and how you will react.

Prioritising your children and knowing that there are ***significant long-term impacts*** for your children if they are exposed to conflict, including manipulative or covert conflict, allows you to make a conscious choice about how you behave and how you manage the behaviour of your ex, working together to find stability for your children as quickly as possible.

Working through your budget ***and understanding your financial position*** and the likely expenses you will incur allows you to make a conscious choice about having the money you need to manage your divorce and plan for the future.

Knowing the importance of *looking after your mind, body, and spirit* and making a conscious choice to prioritise your well-being will enable you to make it through your divorce process and out the other side.

Avoiding game-playing or recognising behaviours that see you avoiding the issues or seeking revenge allows you to make a conscious choice to move through the conflict, communicate well, and make good divorce decisions.

Shifting your attitude to a positive mindset and accepting your role in the separation allows you to make a conscious choice to move forward through the divorce with grace.

Talking to helpful people and seeking advice, especially legal advice, *early on* so that you can make a conscious choice to be empowered by information will enable you to make strategic divorce decisions.

Follow the basic rules – *do the right thing; don't react, act; and pick your battles* – allowing you to make a conscious choice to "play fair" for the benefit of your own well-being.

Finally, know that the rollercoaster ride will end and sideshow alley will close – *the future is yours* – because you have consciously chosen hope, faith, love and joy, made good decisions, and managed your divorce well.

You are going to be just fine.

Acknowledgments

I love writing, and it seems I can't stop. I love creating what I hope are helpful guides for people going through the family law system. My first two books, **Trust Yourself: How Empowered Decision Making Will Help You Resolve Your Family Law Matter** and **Love Law: What to know before you say "I do"**, guide families navigating the family law and estate planning systems in Australia. **Divorce by Design: Empowering yourself through conscious choices** is my first book beyond the Australian shores, and I hope that it has turned out to be a helpful guide if you are contemplating or going through a divorce, regardless of where you live.

Thank you to my clients and the families I have the privilege of helping every day as a lawyer.

Thank you to Ann Dettori and her publishing team at Post Pre-press – if you aren't sure about the self-publishing journey, talk to Ann and work with her to bring your author journey alive.

And thank you to my family and my husband, Fraser, for supporting me in all the random ideas I come up with and, most importantly, for quiet writing time.

Author Contact Details

Elizabeth Fairon is a Legal Practice Director at Life Law Solutions, a law practice in Australia. You can contact Elizabeth at either her Brisbane or Sunshine Coast office as follows:

P: 07 3343 9522 or 07 5446 1745
Email: mail@lifelaw.com.au
Web: www.lifelaw.com.au
LinkedIn: @elizabethfairon

www.ingramcontent.com/pod-product-compliance
Lightning Source LLC
Chambersburg PA
CBHW051435290426
44109CB00016B/1563